What
Works

For

Men

Regaining Lost Ground

You can't change where you've been, but you can change where you're going!

What Works for Men

Published by *El Paseo Publications*

Cover design, Interior design, and Composition by *Scan Communications Group, Inc., Dubuque, IA*

Produced by *Central Plains Book Manufacturing, Winfield, KS*

All biblical references, unless specified otherwise, were obtained from the Spirit Filled Life Bible (New King James version). Executive editor Pastor Jack Hayford. Published by THOMAS NELSON, 1995.
Verses marked NIV are taken from the Holy Bible: New International Version ®.
NIV ®. Copyright © 1973, 1978, 1984 by the International Bible Society.
Verses marked KJV are taken from the King James Version of the Bible.
Verses marked NLT are taken from the New Living Translation. Copyright © 1996 by Tyndale Charitable Trust.
Verses marked NASB are taken from the New American Standard Bible. Copyright © 1960, 1962, 1963, 1968, 1971, 1972, 1973, 1975, 1977, 1995 by the Lockman Foundation.
(Scriptures within quotation marks are exact quotes. Paraphrased Scriptures are noted as such, or are italicized.)

We make every effort to attribute the source of quotes to the correct author. If there is no acknowledgement, the author either wrote the quote or we could not determine the source. If you can identify the source, we encourage you to contact us.

ISBN: 0-9713393-3-3

Library of Congress Control Number:

Printed in the United States of America
10 9 8 7 6 5 4 3 2 1

The What Works Book Series

Book #3

E.P.

EL PASEO PUBLICATIONS
www.elpaseopublications.com

What Works for Men was written based on personal experience and observation, and is sold with that understanding. The purpose of this resource is not to replace other books containing similar information, but to complement them. The Bible provides the primary source of information. Several of the concepts in this book can also be found in *What Works for Singles*; however, the overall content was changed to address the specific needs of men.

   El Paseo Publications is committed to quality in publication—to inspire, educate and encourage the highest standard of excellence through written communication.

ADDITIONAL QUOTES

"*What Works for Men* will be a blessing to every man who reads it; it will help you become aware of your purpose and strengthen your faith. It will challenge you to step to the next level and seek the knowledge & blessings that God has placed inside of you. This book is a spiritual footnote reminding us that we are the '*head and not the tail.*'"
Elder Roger Haley
Activities Manager
The Potter's House Church, Dallas, TX

"*Promise Keepers,* worldwide, is dedicated to building men of integrity and character. *What Works for Men* supports our vision and emphasizes how positive choices, properly prioritized, are woven into God's plan for men. Any man willing to put into practice the principles found in this book will clearly develop integrity and bring glory to God."
Ron Hannah
Senior Vice President of Operations, Promise Keepers Canada

"This book is a great resource for men who desire 'real' change in their lives. I especially appreciate Shane's transparency and the book's practical approach. *What Works for Men* offers great principles with easy to understand steps to growth; I am encouraging men to read it."
Rick Lancaster
Associate Pastor; Family Ministries
Calvary Chapel Menifee

"America would be a better place today if men took their rightful place before God; *What Works for Men* has added more light for men to walk by. Shane Idleman reminds the reader that God's Word is a light for all men for all time."
Pastor Mike MacIntosh
Horizon Christian Fellowship (Calvary Chapel)
San Diego, CA

"Shane Idleman has captured the essence of what problems exist when the world infiltrates the minds of men. He sets forth a 'no-nonsense' approach to overcoming the issues men face today. This book is filled with practical anecdotes that will cause readers to ponder their lifestyles, and ultimately move them into action. I recommend this book to all men—to those in the midst of a struggle, in helping them overcome, and to those whose walk is straight and narrow, to reinforce their walk."

Brad Ormonde
Associate Pastor (Men's Ministry)
Harvest Christian Fellowship, *Greg Laurie—Senior Pastor*
Riverside, CA

"*What Works for Men* is packed full of tools men can use to overcome many of the battles they face today. It is practical, complete with Scripture and is centered on living a victorious Christian life. It is an excellent read . . . and a good re-read—it can be used for men's Bible studies and as a daily devotional; I highly recommend this resource."

Chuck Price—Pastor of Men's Ministry
College Avenue Baptist Church
San Diego, CA

"A book not just of words but action. Shane has captured not only the essence of man and the struggles he faces through life, but shows us how to re-discover God's direction and purpose for it. I strongly recommend this book for individual or small group study and encouragement. May you be re-awakened to the insights of God and His power in your life as you dare to let Him guide you!"

Rod Readhead, C.E.O., Promise Keepers UK

"In reading Shane's book, you cannot help but to see his heart and the way he communicates the issues that men need to hear for such a time as this."

Raul Ries
Calvary Chapel Golden Springs
Diamond Bar, CA

"*What Works for Men* is a down-to-earth, practical and doable guide to becoming a man of character. It's clear that Shane believes in a comprehensive approach to healthy living, physically and spiritually, and both begin with a long-term commitment to Jesus Christ. This book is an excellent resource for those who truly want to change from the inside out."

Dr. Donald E. Wildmon & Tim Wildmon
Chairmen, *American Family Association*

ABOUT THE AUTHOR: *SHANE IDLEMAN*

In just a few short years, Shane Idleman, has written a compelling, biblically-based book series. What makes his story so inspiring is that Idleman had a promising career as a Corporate Executive with the world's fastest growing fitness company, but he left it behind to fulfill a dream God placed within his heart after he recommitted his life to Christ. In his words: *"While I had focused on prosperity, wealth and success, I had starved my soul. I had been independent, self-centered, and prideful. I focused on everything the world had to offer, but ultimately I found that it offered little of lasting value."* When asked why he thought his books are being so well received, he added: *"The overwhelming response simply reflects the need we all have for the truths found in God's Word . . . The books are encouraging, and designed to help the reader stay focused on the goal, not the challenge. . . ."*

Shane's books have sparked change in the lives of many. He's calling marriages, families, and the country back to the values and standards that once made America prized among nations. His bold stance for integrity and morality has led to speaking engagements at some of the largest churches in the nation.

Although physical health has been Shane's primary focus—promoting spiritual health is his greatest desire. His passion for God's Word may well have been planted nearly 400 years ago when the Pilgrims first set foot on American soil. Interestingly enough, Shane's maternal grandfather's lineage can be traced to Peregrine White, the first baby born on the Mayflower in Cape Cod Bay. As the *Mayflower Compact* was signed, members present no doubt prayed that God would bless America, and that their children and grandchildren would carry biblical principles into each new generation. Shane not only believes that his desire to uphold God-given spiritual absolutes in this generation is God's desire for each of us, but, more personally, it may be in answer to that prayer spoken nearly 400 years ago in the early hours of American history.

Today, God's wisdom has all but been removed from social norms. Scripture requires that we stand on our commitments, on our integrity and on our values. Idleman states that many believe that the battle is too advanced, and that we can't make a difference. He believes that we can reverse the trend, and offers this book as his contribution to that commitment.

As a Southern California corporate executive, Shane had opportunity to work with, and oversee hundreds of men. *Challenges varied, however fundamental principles of success did not change.* For many, the ability to look beyond their circumstances and regain lost ground depended largely on the strength of their foundation. From this experience, and his own, Shane isolated several biblical principles that can help us overcome many of the obstacles we face today.

THE AUTHOR'S ACKNOWLEDGMENTS

As mentioned in my first two books, I thank God for inspiration and guidance. As I look back over the years, I'm reminded of II Corinthians 4:8-9: "We are hard-pressed on every side, yet not crushed; we are perplexed, but not in despair; persecuted, but not forsaken; struck down, but not destroyed." When I was hard pressed, I was molded into the person He intended me to be. When I was perplexed, I had only to ask for direction and move forward. When I was persecuted, I found hope through spiritual truths. When I was struck down, clearly God restored me, and when I wanted to give up, I found the endless encouragement to continue.

My mother, Diane Idleman, has continued to offer guidance, encouragement, leadership, integrity and an overall positive attitude toward challenges. When I found myself in battles difficult to face, it was her compassion, understanding and constant reference to God's Word that preserved me. Not only is she a great mother, but an *exceptional* editor and "book doctor." Thank you for the many days, nights, weeks and months invested—may it return a hundred fold. Aside from the Lord, in the words of Abraham Lincoln, *"All that I am, and all that I'll ever be, I owe to my mother!"*

A special thanks to my brother, Ryan, and his wife Christina, along with Christian and Austin, as well as my sister Meredith— all have been a tremendous support. Challenges created by the *What Works Book Series* have brought us closer together. I thank God for family members who add to life rather than take from it.

I also want to thank my wife, Morgan Idleman, who was a tremendous support as I wrote the *What Works Book Series*. Her unconditional love provided stability and strength through ongoing challenges. Thank you for believing in me and in the series—you are truly a blessing. I also want to thank Morgan's family for their support and acceptance: Augie, Linda, Leah, Curt, Jessica and Allison.

I began by acknowledging my heavenly Father and it seems fitting to end with my biological father. Jim Idleman, who died of a heart attack at an early age of fifty-four, inspired me more than he could have known. Qualities such as honesty, integrity, commitment, discipline and a very strong work ethic are not easily taught. *Values are not transmitted through mere words; they are instilled through a life that models these traits.* I learned many things through his example, and I'll be forever grateful for the experiences we shared, the lessons I learned and the man I became as a result of the time we spent together.

Though not aware of their influence via the media, several others have provided spiritual fortification and fuel for the completion of this book. My thanks to James Dobson, Billy & Franklin Graham, Roger Haley, Jack Hayford, Bishop Jakes, James MacDonald, Chuck Smith, Charles Stanley, Chuck Swindoll, Zig Ziglar, and those on The Calvary Satellite Network, The Living Way Radio Network, Focus on the Family, Family Life Today, and Promise Keepers, to name only a few.

EDITORIAL OVERVIEW

Diane Idleman, the author's mother, who was extremely instrumental in the success of the *What Works Book Series*, provides the editorial and advisory overview of the book. She received a Bachelors and Masters Degree in Psychology, and adds several years of experience in working with families and couples in crisis in Southern California. She is also a certified teacher for the University of Phoenix. Thus, the series of books draws on years of practical experience as well as professional knowledge.

Morgan Idleman, the author's wife, provided additional insight and overview during the editing and content revision stages.

CONTENTS

BEGIN HERE

Whether single, married or divorced, all of us have made mistakes and have probably fallen short of our hopes and expectations. God's Word provides direction and encouragement through challenges and tough decisions; thus, a large portion of *What Works for Men* draws from biblical principles and is intended to inspire and motivate. As you read, when you notice areas that require change, I encourage you to simply take the necessary steps and begin to make those changes. While writing this book, areas in my own life surfaced that required attention; I committed to work on them as well. Together we'll make this journey and together we will succeed!

As you begin, I strongly encourage you to journal. Journaling is an excellent way to give place to thoughts, release emotions and to help chart progress. Reflect on your notes and identify areas that may require more attention. For those interested, I've included a section for journaling in the back of the book. God placed great emphasis on the written word as well as the spoken word. Choose a subject, perhaps on developing your character. Find related Scriptures and read the chapters in their entirety. Date your entry; note the Scripture, your thoughts, prayers and how it can be directly applied to your life. Note answers to prayers. You'll be encouraged as you reflect on God's provision throughout your life.

The foundation we build today
provides the strength that weathers
the storm tomorrow.

CHAPTER ONE

Principle

Humility—Choosing to Change from the Inside Out

Change Your Life and It Will Change You

THE MOST IMPORTANT DECISION

I remember it as if it were yesterday. It was the summer of 2000. I was a corporate executive in Southern California for the world's fastest growing fitness company and I had just concluded a phone call with the president of the *Central California division* of our operations. He was generating a year-end report for the board of directors and needed to know how much revenue my area would generate in the last quarter of 2000. Instead of answering his question, I responded, "I need to speak with you about my future with this corporation." He insisted that I drive to the corporate office and meet with him later that day.

As I drove, I reflected on my eight-year career. It was amazing that I had made it this far—a country boy working in corporate America. I had learned well through my dad's example—long hours and hard work, and I applied them. During the first six years of my career, I received awards, set sales records, received large bonuses and climbed the corporate ladder; I was living the "American Dream" (all while in my mid and late twenties). But I wasn't meeting with the President to talk about future opportunities; I was meeting with him to resign.

This may not have made sense to my friends and colleagues, but to me it made perfect sense. For years I was driven, but for the wrong reasons. Although I felt a sense of purpose, it often left me feeling empty. I was passionate, but for the wrong things. I focused on everything society had to offer, but ultimately I found that it offered little of lasting value. While I had focused on money, status and recognition, I had starved other important areas of my life, including my relationship with God. Due to my misguided focus, my life took many turns for the worse.

In 1998, desperate for direction and fulfillment, I began to search the pages of a Bible shelved long ago. As I read, two Scriptures seemed to leap from the pages: "For what profit is it to a man if he gains the whole world, and is himself destroyed or lost?" (Luke 9:25), and ". . . Today, if you will hear His voice, do not harden your hearts" (Hebrews 4:7). I realized that I had been looking for fulfillment in all the wrong places. It was then that I finally recommitted my life to Christ. I quickly learned that before meaningful, lasting change can occur on the outside, it first must occur on the inside. We cannot successfully change actions and circumstances without first changing the inner condition of our heart—we must humbly *choose to change from the inside out.* Just as investing in physical exercise builds and strengthens the body, ongoing spiritual investments build and strengthen our relationship with God. In the fitness industry, for example,

> *Before meaningful, lasting change can occur on the outside, it first must occur on the inside.*

the majority of those who lose weight from dieting gain it back—they don't make an ongoing investment in a lifestyle that promotes health and fitness. *A temporary solution cannot solve a long-term problem.* Regardless if weight is lost through dieting or pills, if the core of the problem is not addressed, success is difficult to maintain. In the same way, if we don't address thoughts, attitudes and behavioral patterns that hinder a successful life, long-term fulfillment is not likely.

One redeeming, yet largely unacknowledged fact of life, is that our past does not have to determine our present or our future—*a true measure of a person is not who they were, but who they will become.* Yes, there are consequences to our actions, but past failures do not have to prevent future success. In fact, many successful people have replaced the concept of "failure" with a more positive concept of "feedback." Don't misunderstand . . . if failure is related to sin, it's wrong, but God wants us to move forward in forgiveness, rather than remain imprisoned by regret.

> *God wants us to move forward in forgiveness, rather than remain imprisoned by regret.*

It was sobering when I finally read, for the first time with open eyes, Matthew 7:22, "Many will say to Me in that day, 'Lord, Lord have we not prophesied in Your name, cast out demons in Your name, and done many wonders in Your name?'" And He will say "*. . . I never knew you; depart from Me, you who practice lawlessness*" (7:23 italics mine). Some might say that they don't understand how Jesus can say, "I never knew you." He's not denying their existence; He's denying a personal relationship with them. It became very clear when I applied it to my life, "But Lord, Lord . . . I attended church on the days that I didn't play golf, or go to the gym, or sleep in, and I was basically a good person." The answer was the same, "I never knew you." As an example, I can watch my favorite team on television, read the players' biographies and study their stats, but if I were to meet them, they would say, "I don't know you." *Knowing about someone is not knowing someone.* A relationship is built when it becomes a priority. Christ has designed the way to develop a relationship with Him: continually read His Word, pray and seek His will for your life by walking in obedience. I've walked on both sides of the fence and there's no comparison.

Matthew 7:19-21 adds extra insight: "Every tree that does not bear good fruit is cut down and thrown into the fire. Therefore by their fruits you will know them. Not everyone who says to Me, 'Lord, Lord,' shall enter the kingdom of heaven, *but he who does the will of My Father in heaven*" (italics mine). I asked myself, "Is it possible for a person to verbally accept Christ and not be saved if there is no evident change in their lifestyle?" I've heard varying opinions on the subject, but I will say this: if you sense that your relationship with Jesus is shallow and incomplete, it probably is. I encourage you to revisit your commitment and understand that accepting Christ isn't the finishing line; it's the starting point. When we genuinely accept Him, there should be a complete change in the way we live our lives, or, at least, a strong desire to do so. If there isn't a significant change and/or a desire to serve Him, our relationship may be superficial, and that is not a good place to be.

> *Accepting Christ isn't the finishing line; it's the starting point.*

Eventually, I had to accept the fact that I was a sinner who needed a Savior before I could truly change from the inside out. I stopped blaming people, places or things and started taking responsibility for my actions from an inward position, and began moving in a positive direction.

Turning Point Ministries describes four emotional states that can prevent change.

1. The first is *blame* (feeds denial). When we fail to take responsibility for our actions, the endless cycle of blame, anger and un-forgiveness often continues. Those enslaved by blame and un-forgiveness are truly imprisoned, and the walls they build to protect them may eventually imprison them. If this is you, as it was me, I encourage you to remove blame, resentment and/or bitterness from your life. These destructive forces do nothing but add extra weight to the journey.

2. Second is *resentment* (anger at the situation). It's been said that *life makes us better or it makes us bitter;* it's our choice. If anger causes damage to our character, or damage to another, it is not accomplishing God's purpose. By holding on to anger, we jeopardize our health and the health of our family, not to mention the psychological damage it causes.

> *The walls they build to protect them may eventually imprison them.*

3. Third is *rationalization* (making excuses for actions). By excusing our actions, we deny responsibility. Those who continue with harmful addictions, for example, often excuse their actions and even justify them. Take responsibility, even if it hurts initially.

4. The fourth state is *hopelessness* (the result of a perceived helpless condition). Hopelessness often occurs when we've been defeated in a certain area. Many fail to move forward because they are hindered by their emotional state of hopelessness. They must release this attitude before they can move forward. *Without an inward change in thoughts, an outward change in actions is unlikely.* Choosing to change your lifestyle from the inside out begins with a choice. Choosing today changes tomorrow!

You may be saying, "Where is this going?" Straight to the point: without Jesus Christ truly leading the way, all efforts will be in vain. It's often been said that *sin takes us farther than we want to go, costs us more than we want to pay and keeps us longer than we want to stay.* I couldn't agree more. Many men go through life pursuing dreams that never come true, chasing things that can never be caught and living with past pain that never heals. Accepting a new life in Christ changes that. II Corinthians 5:17 states: "Therefore, if anyone is in Christ, he is a new creation; old things have passed away; behold, all things have become new." Your past is forgiven, your present secure and your future certain; through Christ you are a new person.

Jesus has made Himself available to us. He gave us the ability to think, to reason and to choose to accept Him or reject Him. I believe that life is an

> *Your past is forgiven, your present secure and your future certain.*

intentional act; it is not the result of a random cosmic explosion that organized itself into magnificent life. God didn't create anything without a purpose. If life is a gift, then there's a Giver. If we were created, then there's a Creator. If there is a master plan, then there's a Master Planner. It would be a waste of precious time not to allow God to direct our lives.

If you're reading this and are skeptical because of past experiences with religion, that's okay; religion is not the answer— *a relationship with Christ* is. There is a clear difference.

➤ Religion says, "I have to follow rules." A relationship with Christ says, "I want to follow His plan for my life."

➤ Religion says, "I have to go to church." A relationship with Christ says, "I want to position myself to learn more, worship Him and benefit from fellowship."

➤ Religion offers a set of rituals; a relationship with Jesus offers a guiding light.

➤ Religion is man's attempt to find God; relationship assures us of His presence.

I believe that many "Christian" men (and women) lose sight of their purpose because they have "religion" and not a true relationship with Christ. They may know Scripture but they often do not apply it to their lives.

One of the most dangerous statements we can make is, "I know what God's Word says, *but . . .*" For example:

I know that I shouldn't watch that movie or television program, *but* I enjoy it.

I know that I shouldn't date her, *but* she's very attractive.

I know that I shouldn't go there, *but* everyone is doing it.

I know what Jesus said, *but* this is what He really meant.

I know what the Bible says, *but* it doesn't apply now.

I know that I need to go to church, pray and read God's Word, *but* I'm too busy.

When we run contrary to God's principles, we disregard the very thing that was designed to guide and protect us. We have faith in banks, businesses, vehicles, buildings and friends, but when it comes to having

> *Consider God's guidelines as guardrails through the canyons of life.*

faith in an all-knowing, all-powerful God, we seem to have trouble. Consider God's guidelines as guardrails through the canyons of life.

Many also have difficulty relating to Jesus and believing in Him; they don't understand why God sent His Son. Working closely with my father helped me better understand this truth. Many times, as a teen, I assisted him throughout the day. He owned a construction company that specialized in the installation of underground services. At times, I would jump into a five, six or seven foot deep trench to install a new pipeline. Five minutes into the installation, it was obvious that I was at a loss. From above, my dad would give me helpful orders like, "Stop! Do it this way," or "Don't do it like that, you'll break the pipe." After many attempts to help me from his position above, he would inevitably jump down into the trench and show me how to do my job successfully. It wasn't until he came down to my level, demonstrated the proper technique, and explained the process that I fully understood. Although not perfect, I made vast improvements as the training sessions continued. In the same way, Jesus was sent to teach us how to lead godly, meaningful lives and to "save us from ourselves." In essence, the price was so great, that at the end of His ministry, Jesus paid the highest price of all by dying to redeem us from our sins.

The greatest commitment that you will ever make is to continually develop and guard your spiritual health—a half-hearted approach will not work. *If you're searching but not finding, hurting and not healing, and living but not loving, I encourage you to first look to the One who has the answers and commit your life to Him.*

One of the reasons why many men do not humble themselves and surrender their lives to Christ is because the enemy deceives us into believing that embracing the Christian faith is for those who are weak. Society tells us to do things "our way"—to be strong, domineering and forceful.

In my early twenties, I believed that I was a man because I could bench press over four hundred pounds, drink a twelve pack of beer and win most of the fights that I was in. I failed to realize that I was weak inside. I didn't have control of my desires—my desires had control of me.

Years later, I began to read more about the life of Christ. It was obvious that I was completely wrong about Christianity. Who, but Jesus, would say, *no man takes my life; I lay it down* (John 10:18). Who, but Jesus, would say to Pontius Pilate when confronted with death, "You would have no power over me at all unless it were given to you from above . . ." (John 19:11 NLT). Who, but Jesus, when hanging on a cross, severely beaten and dying for our sins, would say of his accusers, ". . . Father, forgive them; for they know not what they do . . ." (Luke 23:34 KJV). Christianity does not represent weakness; it represents meekness. *Weakness is the absence of strength; meekness is strength under control.* It takes far more strength to be a man of God than to lead a life void of His presence.

> *It takes far more strength to be a man of God than to lead a life void of His presence.*

To carry the weight of responsibility as husbands, leaders and fathers we must continually focus on building and strengthening our foundation (e.g., our character and relationship with Christ). Unmistakably, the foundation we build today provides the strength that weathers the storm tomorrow.

It's unfortunate that today's society focuses largely on external factors (e.g., money, position, and status). These superficial values have left our nation in a moral, as well as a spiritual crisis. *We've become a society focused on prosperity instead of provision, we value wealth instead of wisdom and we are drawn to charisma instead of character.* Our foundation as a nation, and as individuals, has slowly deteriorated, but that can be changed if we once again focus on God's Word and biblical principles, and live our lives accordingly.

WATER THE ROOTS

Many of our nation's founders and early leaders built our nation on biblical principles. They recognized spiritual truths fundamental for ". . . life, liberty and the pursuit of happiness." For example, the school system was created to teach God's Word, and the legal system was based on the Ten Commandments.

I'm a firm believer that *if we don't water the roots, the plants will die.* I grew up in Southern California and was trained by a mother who had a passion for seasonal flowers and chore charts. My job one summer, in addition to others, was watering the flowerpots that lined our front and back patios. It was a simple job, but I was easily bored and anxious to get on with other things. After quickly sprinkling the plants for several days, most of the flowers withered and died. Rather than a lecture, mom felt that the best way to teach responsibility and the need to soak the roots, was to have me replace the flowers from my allowance. I learned a valuable lesson: *keep the roots alive.* In the same way, if we fail to keep America's spiritual roots alive, we may lose a rich harvest of God's blessing.

Nearly four hundred years ago, English Puritans set sail for a land where God's ordinances would govern, and America was born. At that time, our Founding Fathers understood the wisdom in God's directives for a prosperous life. In William Martin's book, *A Prophet with Honor—The Billy Graham Story,* he recalls John Cotton's warning to the Puritans . . . "as soon as God's Ordinances cease, your Security ceaseth likewise; but if God plant his Ordinances among you, fear not, he will maintain them." In other words, when we fail to cultivate God's Word, our security, defense and protection can cease, yet God will continue to call from each generation those who will support His laws (i.e., ordinances); I believe that we, you and I, are called in this generation to support these truths.

Our country's motto has been "IN GOD WE TRUST," and our national mindset reflected Christian values. Sadly, today's culture often promotes *relativism* and man does what is right in his own eyes—abortion and divorce are now determined by personal preference rather than by God's Word. Pornography is commonly protected as an expression of free speech, while school prayer is often banned. Our society clearly reflects man's digression from God; our nation's current culture cannot produce safe, secure living. Fortunately, for those who follow Christ, He promises peace amidst the storm.

Where do you stand on abortion, purity, honesty, commitment and respect for others? Do you accept the secular philosophy that what feels right is right, or do you follow biblical principles? For those who may be skeptical, let me present one question: if the Bible is the Word of God, and if moral absolutes were given to guide, direct and protect mankind, where will the enemy center his attack? You got it . . . *in the area of moral absolutes.*

As previously mentioned, America's present philosophy of relativism/secular humanism runs contrary to God's wisdom and is spreading throughout education, government and the justice system, largely by those who were educated by this philosophy in the 1960's and somewhat earlier. Those schooled by secular humanism have greatly influenced legislation and cultural values. The transition from God-centered principles to man-centered values is a spiritual war deliberately waged by the adversary.

There was a time in our recent history when America felt secure knowing that its most formidable enemies were abroad. Today, our nation is threatened by relentless enemies both foreign and within.

I'm reminded of the story of a young girl who wrote this letter: "Dear God, why did You allow armed students to walk into a school and open fire on the students?" He replied, *"Dear little girl, because I'm no longer allowed in schools."* Removing God from our country is as tragic as removing Him from our schools.

It is sobering to think that today's students will be tomorrow's leaders. Fortunately, there are young people rising who are passionate about personal and national integrity based on absolutes. If this is you, I encourage you to continue; you will make a difference!

I once heard a news commentator discuss terrorist activity in the Middle East and how we can prepare for future attacks. The commentator then turned attention to the problem in corporate America; he stated that Americans are losing trust in large companies because of inflated profit margins and lack of ethical principles. It struck me that while we are concerned with terrorist attacks, and rightly so, there is a greater threat from corruption within. America's blessings are simply the fruit of yesterday's past. There is a saying: *one generation plants trees for the next generation.* I am concerned that, rather than planting, we are tearing them down and removing the very covering that protects us.

> *America's blessings are simply the fruit of yesterday's past.*

As Christians, we are called to lead our families, our communities and our nation within a framework of spiritual principles, guided by humility. *Choosing to change from the inside out* not only involves our commitment to Christ, but to our families and our country as well. We are directed to hold fast to our commitments, to our integrity and to our values. Don't be fooled by thinking you can't make a difference—you can; society changes as individuals change! We are to believe in God, accept His Son, exhibit faith and walk with integrity. M.H. McKee states it well, "Integrity is one of several paths. It distinguishes itself from the others because it is the right path, and the only one upon which you will never get lost." Are you holding on to your integrity and choosing the right path? If not, you can change that today.

> *Don't be fooled by thinking you can't make a difference—you can; society changes as individuals change!*

CHANGING DIRECTION

Choosing to change is the first step and the most important. As you begin, remember that a strong foundation will cost you

A strong foundation will cost you something, but a weak foundation can cost you everything.

something, but a weak foundation can cost you everything. If you are choosing to accept Christ as your personal Savior for the first time, continue to build on solid ground. Psalm 11:3 states, "If the foundations are destroyed, what can the righteous do?" and Isaiah 7:9 states, ". . . if you do not stand firm in your faith, you will not stand at all" (NIV). These Scriptures are to encourage and to illustrate the importance of continually building your faith on God's Word.

No matter what you've done or have been through, you have the ability and availability to accept or return to Jesus and become as new. Again, a true measure of a man is not who he was, but who he will become. Simply . . .

. . . acknowledge that Jesus died for your sins (John 3:16)

. . . acknowledge that you are a sinner in need of a Savior (Rom 3:23)

. . . repent and turn from your sins (Acts 3:19)

. . . live your life for Him (II Corinthians 5:15)

Strengthen your foundation by . . .

1. Finding a Bible believing, Christ-centered church, and attend often.

2. Avoiding looking outside of the Bible for so-called "deeper truths" or "broader meanings"; you won't find them.

3. Avoiding mixing religions. Jesus said, ". . . I am the way, the truth, and the life: no man cometh unto the Father, but by me" (John 14:6 KJV).

4. Devoting a portion of your day to prayer.

5. Purchasing a good study Bible; read and journal.

6. Memorizing Bible Scriptures and use them as a standard for direction and decision.

7. Developing relationships with those who will encourage you to grow in your faith.

8. Listening often to Christ-centered, biblically based radio programs.

Special Note: For many years, when a book or resource was recommended to me, especially the Bible, I often said, "No thanks, I'm not a reader." But when I recommitted my life to Christ, something changed. I studied the Bible daily, listened to countless hours of sermons and read dozens of Christian books. Looking back, the reason I avoided reading the Bible was because my spirit was sick. In the medical industry, *hunger is often a sign of health.* In the same way, our spiritual hunger is related to our spiritual health. If there is a lack of hunger for God's Word and spiritual growth, the spirit is weak and may be sick. Many men wouldn't dream of avoiding food all day, let alone all week; why then do we often neglect spiritual food, which is vastly more important?

I cannot stress enough the importance of reading God's Word daily—it is the lifeline to the failing spiritual health of our nation.

—"Blessed are those who hunger and thirst for righteousness, for they shall be filled" (Matthew 5:6).—

The obstacles ahead are never
greater than God's power
to take you through.

CHAPTER TWO

Principle

Acquire Knowledge

What You Don't Know "Can" Hurt You

As stated earlier, many of my teen years and early twenties were spent working for our family's construction company. One morning while I was digging a trench with a backhoe, I broke an existing water line. Within minutes, the trench filled with water. I rushed to shut off the valve, but the handle appeared to be broken. I struggled to close it with a screwdriver, a pair of pliers and other wrenching tools, but nothing worked. Hesitantly, I called my dad to tell him that I couldn't stop hundreds of gallons of water from pouring into the street. When he arrived, clearly frustrated, he reached into his truck and grabbed a long pole with a special socket attached. As he placed the socket on the so-called "broken valve" and turned it; the water stopped immediately. He reminded me, not so patiently, of his words just weeks prior. He had instructed me to keep the special wrench with me at all times for emergencies like this.

I learned two important lessons. First, I received proper instruction, but I failed to listen to my father's advice. Had I used the right tool, the damage, if any, would have been minimal. In the same way, biblical principles and godly wisdom are available to us, but it's our choice whether we use them or not. I thought I had other options, the pliers, screwdriver and other tools seemed as if they would work; I felt I could manage without the water-meter wrench, but my failure to heed my father's advice cost us the price of the job. In the same way, we often think of "our way" as best and God's principles as optional when, in fact, the opposite is true: God's directives are essential and absolute.

> *Biblical principles and godly wisdom are available to us, but it's our choice whether we use them or not.*

Second, I realized that I could not fix the problem alone and called for my father's help. Likewise, we all encounter problems, and need to ask for help even when problems are self-created. Calling on our Heavenly Father should be the first resort, not the last. Had I called my father first—or listened initially—the damage would have been considerably less. In the same way, heed the *right* advice and look to the *right* source for help in building a foundation of knowledge in your life.

Timeless tips

Although the entire Bible provides knowledge, wisdom and guidance for difficult decisions, the following pages contain timeless tips from the book of Proverbs. Proverbs 1:4 (NLT) states . . . "These Proverbs will make the simpleminded clever. They will give knowledge and purpose to young people." God promises that reading and applying His Word to our lives will give us wisdom and purpose; however, reading alone doesn't guarantee success, application does. Difficult

> *Reading alone doesn't guarantee success, application does.*

and challenging decisions become less complicated when they are based on Scripture. God's Word enables, empowers and endorses success. It provides the energy to deal with life's challenges and the strength to press through regardless of circumstances. Many often say that they just need to get their lives together before they commit to biblical principles. If this is you, don't wait until that time to apply God's Word to your life—you may wait a lifetime. Start now, regardless of your current situation. *Those who succeed walk through adversity, not without it.* There's no "best" time to start. Simply start now and remember that as long as you take two steps forward, even after stepping back, you'll continue to move in the right direction.

(Unless specified otherwise, the following Scriptures are taken from the New Living Translation Bible or the New King James Bible.)

Build the foundation of knowledge by . . .

<u>Fearing the Lord</u>
Proverbs 1:7 . . . **"The fear of the Lord is the beginning of knowledge, but fools despise wisdom and instruction."** The fear of the Lord is where it all must start. This isn't the type of fear that one may have toward an abusive parent, but rather, one that is born out of respect and reverence for God. Fear, in this sense, causes us to dread the consequence of walking in disobedience to His Word.

Fearing the Lord leads to wisdom, and wisdom and knowledge are incredibly important for a successful life. Proverbs 4:7-8 states, "Wisdom is the principle thing; therefore get wisdom. And in all your getting, get understanding. Exalt her and she will promote you; she will bring you honor, when you embrace her."

<u>Walking In Integrity</u>
Proverbs 2:7 . . . **"He grants a treasure of good sense to the godly. He is their shield, protecting those who walk with integrity."** Proverbs 20:7 adds, "The godly walk with integrity; blessed are their children after them." Walking in integrity not only affects you, but those around you as well. Proverbs 10:9

concludes . . . "People with integrity have firm footing, but those who follow crooked paths will slip and fall." Integrity is a key ingredient when it comes to leading a godly life, and it should be at the forefront of every decision. A good way to measure your level of integrity is to ask this simple question: "Am I honest on my taxes, with my wife and on my job?" We should all strive to answer "yes" to these and similar questions.

Seeking and Trusting Him

Proverbs 3:5-6 . . . **"Trust in the Lord with all your heart; do not depend on your own understanding. Seek his will in all you do, and he will direct your paths."** As long as we are walking morally upright and obeying His principles, He will direct us—one way or the other. There is a blessing just beyond the circumstance. Simply trust despite appearances and keep moving forward.

Setting Your Sites

Proverbs 4:25-27 . . . **"Look straight ahead, and fix your eyes on what lies before you. Mark out a straight path for your feet; then stick to the path and stay safe. Don't get sidetracked; keep your feet from following evil."** When I was a teen, my father would often take my brother and me "trap shooting." As soon as clay targets were released from a small building built partially under ground, we'd pull the guns to our shoulders and prepare to fire. There were only seconds to aim and fire as the clay targets darted through the air. If we took our eyes off the target, even for a second, we would miss the shot. The same holds true for our spiritual lives. If we neglect to continually focus on the right path, we can miss the ultimate target—God's most productive plan for our lives.

Building A Successful Marriage

Proverbs 5:18 **". . . Rejoice in the wife of your youth."** Whether married for years or just days, we are to continually celebrate and delight in our wives. Most desire a happy marriage. Unfortunately, desire alone is not enough; it takes action.

Considering the number of men today who want a happy marriage, and that would be most who are married—far too few actually arrive. Why? Many do not make *ongoing* investments in a lifestyle that promotes a healthy marriage.

Love hopes for and believes the best in our wives. We may not always see the best in them, but we trust that it is there and we encourage it to grow. I believe that God often places us with those we can help, and the opposite is also true. *Don't view a challenging marriage as something to run from, but rather as something to run to.* It's not the difficulties in marriage that defeat us—it's generally our attitude and response to the problems that determines whether we succeed or fail. When life becomes challenging, we often blame our marriage and say, "This isn't working." Marriage never works out—you have to work it out. Anger, resentment, bitterness, frustration and un-forgiveness can produce a negative, unproductive attitude, and have no place in the marriage relationship. Instead of bringing unnecessary baggage into the relationships, we should be lightening the load. We need to learn to pray for our wives rather than to get angry, to understand rather than become impatient and to love unconditionally rather than to walk away. Within this secure and nurturing framework, the marriage can thrive. If you're aware of any issues that may prevent the development of a healthy relationship, I encourage you to begin working on them today and save your marriage before it has a chance to fail. Make a healthy marriage your priority—it will not happen on its own. What it takes to develop and build the relationship is what it takes to keep it going!

> *Marriage never works out—you have to work it out.*

If you are single, remember . . . who you are when single will be who you are when married, at least initially. For this reason, it's vitally important to develop qualities now that you'll want to continue to develop throughout marriage. Marriages that begin with right intentions but end in divorce often fail to continue to nurture and strengthen the relationship.

More on marriage—what you need to know

It's no surprise that more than fifty percent of all marriages in the United States end in divorce. I believe this number would be significantly lower if basic principles were acknowledged before marriage, as well as after. Love doesn't leave people—people leave love. True love is not just an ecstatic feeling; it's a decision that we make to remain faithful to our commitment.

> *Love doesn't leave people—people leave love.*

Marriage was intended to be a commitment based on love, surrendered to service, built on perseverance and held together by commitment. A newsletter from *FOCUS ON THE FAMILY* stated that when a research team studied 5,232 married adults who were interviewed in the late 1980's, they discovered that 645 of them were unhappily married. Five years later, these same adults (some divorced, separated or still married) were interviewed again. The study revealed that two-thirds of the unhappily married spouses who remained together were actually happier five years later. The opposite was true for those divorced. Although divorce was a temporary escape from pain, it introduced new emotional and psychological difficulties. In a nutshell, unless problems are severe and/or life threatening, weather the storm—it's well worth it.

<u>Avoiding Sexual Sin</u>

Proverbs 6:32 . . . **"But the man who commits adultery is an utter fool, for he destroys his own soul."** Adultery not only pertains to the physical act, it can refer to our thought life as well. Jesus said in Matthew 5:28 ". . . that whoever looks at a woman to lust for her has already committed adultery with her in his heart." Adultery, mentally or physically, breaks the bond between a husband and a wife; and the spiritual union of two people was never designed to be broken. Nothing is more detrimental to a marriage than adultery.

Proverbs 9:17-18 provides additional instruction, "Stolen water is sweet, and bread eaten in secret is pleasant. But he does not know that the dead are there, that her guests are in the depths of hell." Please understand that I'm not trying to overwhelm you, but the consequences of sexual sin can be

Many forget that poor choices have long-term consequences.

tragic. If we candy-coat this issue and fail to see it for what it is, we can easily be misled. Unfortunately, many forget that poor choices have long-term consequences. Married or single, if you sense that you're heading in the wrong direction, simply begin to make the necessary lifestyle changes, repent and ask God to re-direct you. *He is faithful to lead those who want to follow.*

Developing A Teachable Spirit

Proverbs 9:9 . . . **"Teach the wise, and they will be wiser. Teach the righteous, and they will learn more."** Embrace "constructive" criticism and learn from the advice of others. God does mighty things in the lives of those who are teachable and humble. Proverbs 18:12 (NIV) adds, "Before his downfall a man's heart is proud, but humility

The "higher" you think you are, the farther you can fall.

comes before honor." Be careful, the "higher" you think you are, the farther you can fall.

During my career in the fitness industry, I had the privilege of overseeing hundreds of employees. Those who had a teachable and positive attitude often excelled and were a pleasure to work with; those filled with pride and negativity rarely lasted more than a few months.

In addition, Proverbs 27:2 states, "Don't praise yourself; let others do it." It's not commendable to point out our accomplishments or income, or even our spiritual growth. God directs us to humble ourselves and not to think more of ourselves than we should. When we are boastful and arrogant, we often appear self-centered—not a very admirable quality. Allow others to congratulate and honor you as you seek to do the same.

Giving Generously

Proverbs 11:25 . . . **"The generous prosper and are satisfied; those who refresh others will themselves be refreshed."** Regardless of what we think, everything we own is God's; our job is to simply take care of what has been given to us. I'm reminded of the story found in Luke 19:11-27. A master gave his servants talents to invest. Two of the servants invested wisely and took care of what had been given to them. The last servant hid the talent and did nothing with it. As a result, he lost it. We, too, are equally entrusted with gifts and freedom with how we are to invest in the lives of others, whether financially, relationally or physically— *God will reward us as we honor others.*

Measuring Your Words

Proverbs 15:1 . . . **"A gentle answer turns away wrath, but harsh words stir up anger,"** and Proverbs 18:21 reminds us, "Death and life are in the power of the tongue . . ." Rethink what you're about to say before you say it. Ask, "Are my words going to build the other person up or tear them down? Negative words, and/or lack of positive words expressed to others can play an enormous role in shaping or reshaping their lives, especially when it comes to what we say to our wives and children. Choose your words carefully and encourage, not discourage, the success of others; and choose your thoughts carefully in promoting your own success.

Exercising Power Through Patience

Proverbs 16:32 . . . **"It is better to be patient than powerful; it is better to have self-control than to conquer a city."** Patient people deliberately take their time and examine the possibilities, weigh the consequences, seek guidance if necessary and do what they believe to be right. Self-control allows us to control our desires and emotions rather than allowing them to control us. *I rarely hear people say, "I moved too slowly," but I often hear, "I moved too quickly."* Slow down—it's worth the wait.

Making Room

Proverbs 18:16 says, **"A man's gift makes room for him . . ."**
God gives each of us gifts to give away. He has called us all to
be part of a large, collective body that ministers to the needs of
others. Some may have gifts of teaching, administration,
preaching or leading. They may have been called to be a
businessman, a technician, a pastor, an actor, etc. Problems
arise when we try to be what we are not. For instance, if God
has called you to work with children and you're spending your
time as a business professional, fulfillment may be hard to
come by. On the other hand, some are doing what they love but
still lack fulfillment, largely because of their definition of
success. For example, a businessman may work exhausting
hours, promote his business religiously and hire the best
employees, but the company doesn't flourish. He sees other
businesses succeeding and wonders why his is not. The
question shouldn't be, "Why am I not succeeding?," but rather,
"Am I pursuing my God-given purpose?" and *"How am I
measuring success?"* Maybe he should redefine success. Is
there a difference between a businessman who makes millions
of dollars each year and whose company is rapidly approaching
the Fortune 500, compared to the businessman who sells just
enough to get by, serves at church and attends to the daily
needs of his wife and children? Society may believe that
there is a huge difference; one is a "success" the other is not.
But God looks at the heart rather than outward appearance
(1 Samuel 16:7). It may be that both are successful in His eyes.
Surely He blesses people with prosperity and recognition, but in
many cases, the one who appears least is actually greater.
Simply ask yourself, *"Am I trying to do my best*, or be the
best?"* Doing your best and being the best can spring from
different motives. When we try to "be the best" we may have
the tendency to compete and compromise our character, thus
lowering our standards in the pursuit of being number one, or
rising to the top. Is it always easy? Not at all! But when we

Strive for excellence and make every effort to accomplish your goals, but check your method and motives.

reflect on just how blessed we are as a nation and how gracious God has been, we can be immediately encouraged and motivated to continue. Strive for excellence and make every effort to accomplish your goals, but check your method and motives.

Trusting His Lead

Proverbs 20:24 . . . **"How can we understand the road we travel? It is the Lord who directs our steps."** We will never fully understand the complexities of life; therefore, trust God and faithfully follow His lead. The Lord directs our steps as we continually look to Him and His Word for guidance.

Taking No Shortcuts to Success

Proverbs 21:5 . . . **"Good planning and hard work lead to prosperity, but hasty shortcuts lead to poverty."** Proverbs 14:23 also states, "In all labor there is profit, but idle chatter leads only to poverty." Labor is another word for *effort*; idle is another word for *inactivity*. In simpler terms, effort produces results; inactivity doesn't! Putting first things first leads to success. Those things in life worth having generally take energy and commitment to achieve. Don't take shortcuts in business, relationships or finances—they often lead to failure. Gambling, pyramid schemes and other risky ventures, may seem harmless on the surface, but they can have devastating consequences. Even if the loss is minimal, it's the principle that matters—God rewards wise decisions.

"The ladder of success works like any other ladder. Very few have climbed it with their hands in their pockets" (Zig Ziglar).

"The ladder of success works like any other ladder. Very few have climbed it with their hands in their pockets" (Zig Ziglar).

Choosing Reputation Over Riches

Proverbs 22:1 . . . **"Choose a good reputation over great riches, for being held in high esteem is better than having silver or gold."** Don't jeopardize reputation for money. If a challenging decision needs to be made, let integrity guide you, not profit. The Bible tells us that we are to profit or yield a return in what we do, but it also clarifies that we are to do it honestly and with correct motives.

Training Your Children

Proverbs 22:6 (NIV) . . . **"Train a child in the way he should go, and when he is old he will not turn from it."** We should educate our children in all areas of life. For example, a complaint I often hear from parents at weight-loss conferences is that their children insist on eating junk food and that there is nothing that can be done. Actually, there is something that can be done. Depending on the age of the children, parents can purchase healthy foods and set a standard to follow in the home—lead by example. Sadly, society's view of nutrition runs contrary to good health. Choosing to follow a healthy lifestyle, regardless of what today's culture promotes, is an important step in teaching children. After all, when we fail to confront, we may appear to confirm. When we fail to confront destructive attitudes and actions, we may confirm them as acceptable; therefore, teaching children often involves loving confrontation.

When we fail to confront, we may appear to confirm.

Avoiding Friendly Fire

Proverbs 18:24 . . . **"There are 'friends' who destroy each other. . . ."** Think for a moment. If you are standing on a wall, is it easier to pull someone up to your level, or to be pulled down to theirs? Without much thought, you conclude that it's easier to be pulled down. Likewise, the downward pull of society is strong, especially when one is not firmly anchored.

The Bible, for example, makes reference to being equally yoked. II Corinthians 6:14 states, "Do not be unequally yoked together with unbelievers. For what fellowship has righteousness with lawlessness? And what communion has light with darkness?" Although this command is crystal clear, many read it with clouded vision. The Bible regularly advises that companions, good or bad, influence character. Some may claim to be Christians but that doesn't mean that they are walking in obedience to God's Word. Look for the fruit that is produced by the individual's lifestyle. It's easy to believe that you'll influence the other person, but often, he or she has the leverage. "He who walks with wise men will be wise, but the companion of fools will be destroyed" (Proverbs 13:20). The pull of society is strong and it takes an enormous amount of energy to maintain an up-hill stride; an unequal yoke adds weight to the climb—we may enjoy the friendship but *we can be wounded as easily by friendly fire as we can by a foe.* If a person doesn't have the qualities you're looking for in a friend, don't lower your standards; keep them high. Many times, the problem isn't that we raise our standard and miss it, it's that we lower it and hit it. Please understand that I am not suggesting that

> *The problem isn't that we raise our standard and miss it, it's that we lower it and hit it.*

Christians only interact with other Christians; we are called to minister to others in all areas of life, but if the association is pulling in the wrong direction, it's time to reconsider the relationship, or at least, establish boundaries.

Countless times in the Old Testament, God warned His people not to be unequally yoked with other nations, and countless times their disregard led to their downfall. Who we associate with may be who we become. *People can either lift you up, or pull you down.* If you're not sure if the person is a positive or negative influence, consider where the relationship is leading you; is it the direction that you want to go? If not, reconsider the relationship.

Pursuing Moderation

Proverbs 23:4 (NIV) . . . **"Do not wear yourself out to get rich; have the wisdom to show restraint."** When I worked in the corporate world, my seventy-hour week was spent crunching numbers, reviewing revenue lines, hitting board allocated budgets and auditing departments. I was not afforded the luxury of being involved in the lives of others to the

Focus on the blessings you do have, not on the things you don't have.

degree that I am now. I had certain protocols and agendas that demanded my time. Ultimately, I gave up so much for so little. Use wisdom and moderation as you pursue your dreams, and focus on the blessings you do have, not on the things you don't have.

Following the Three Keys to Success

Although we've been referencing the book of Proverbs, Psalm 1:1-3 provides three closing points as we continue to build the foundation of knowledge in our lives.

"Blessed is the man who walks not in the counsel of the ungodly, nor stands in the path of sinners, nor sits in the seat of the scornful; but his delight is in the law of the Lord, and in His law he meditates day and night. He shall be like a tree planted by the rivers of water, that brings forth its fruit in its season, whose leaf also shall not wither; and whatever he does shall prosper."

1. *Blessed is the man who walks not in the counsel of the ungodly.* Who do you associate with, listen to or spend time with? Are they encouraging or discouraging you? What do you watch on TV and/or the Internet, or listen to on the radio? What do you read? Simply position yourself correctly to receive God's blessing.

2. *Do not stand in the path of the sinner or sit in the seat of the scornful.* It's hard to get hit by a train if you're not on the tracks. If you're currently walking in the path of sin, remove yourself, ask for forgiveness and choose another path.

   It's hard to get hit by a train if you're not on the tracks.

3. *Blessed are those who delight in and meditate day and night on the Word of God.* We make decisions daily, sometimes minute to minute. Meditating on God's Word helps us to solve problems based on sound principles. Daily Bible study provides the basis for decision-making, encouragement and wise counsel. Meditating on God's Word keeps His standard for living ever before us; it rewards us with stability and peace.

They who obey these Scriptures will be like trees planted by water and will bear fruit in season; their leaves will not wither, and everything they do will prosper. Bearing fruit in season means that some blessings are not always immediate. Figuratively speaking, you don't see a young apple tree bear abundant fruit; the tree would collapse under the weight. Likewise, God prepares and builds so we can hold the weight of His blessing. Can you envision the weight of responsibility that Billy Graham carried as he ministered to millions over his lifetime? He began faithfully in the small things, and his ministry grew. Don't become frustrated if you haven't received what you've been waiting for; God is building and strengthening you. Remain firmly planted and allow God to add to your increase. Most of us will not minister to millions as Dr. Graham has done; however, we are all capable of producing fruit within our daily lives by touching the lives of others, sometimes moment by moment.

We are also told that our leaves will not wither. God brings life to our spirits and we are to be life giving. God sustains us so that we can help sustain others.

Verse three concludes . . . and whatever he does will prosper. Disciplining ourselves to avoid sin and ungodly counsel, combined with meditating and acting upon God's Word, will lead to a prosperous relationship with God, a prosperous marriage, a prosperous family, a prosperous career, a prosperous single life— all a reflection of a prosperous spirit.

A CLOSING NOTE ON SUCCESS

These tips may seem overwhelming but they are designed to build us up—not to break us down. Remember, it is important to build a strong foundation that will support "lasting" change. If the foundation is weak, the structure is not sound.

Life is like a race of endurance, full of endless opportunities and experiences. There are also occasional roadblocks, delays, pitfalls and hurdles. Make no mistake about it—*we win by persevering, by getting up and not giving in, and by following biblical principles.* Successful people build success from failure, and they don't look back—it's not the direction they want to go. Focus on the goal of living a Christ-centered life and not the challenge, and move forward. Successful people often fail more than failures do; they refuse to give up. Few things hurt us more than failing to forgive others or ourselves for past mistakes. Many times, memories haunt and discourage us from moving forward. As a result, people may rate themselves according to who they were, or what they did, not realizing that who they are now and who they will become is far more important. Avoid the "what others say and think" trap, unless it's positive. We often judge ourselves by their standards, failing to recognize that what people may say about us is not who we actually are. Don't let the opinions of others define you!

Society tends to program our looks and actions. Women, as well as young girls, refer to magazines and TV to see how they should dress and act; teenage boys consult TV and the media for role models, and many men measure their self worth by what they have accomplished in business and financially, not realizing that a relationship with God, family and others is the treasure they should be seeking.

Secular values have eroded qualities such as moral integrity, discipline and commitment from today's society, just as water and time have eroded the banks of the Colorado River and left a vast

Grand Canyon. Erosion can occur so slowly that we are unaware until its work is done. It has the power to change the course of a mighty river and it can surely change the course of our lives. Again, *don't allow a declining culture to erode essential qualities in your life.* You can make a difference by following and obeying God's Word. With life we were given power. The power to persevere is one of the greatest attributes that we possess. There is little we can do about life's glitches except to control the way we respond to them. Remember . . . the obstacles ahead are not greater than God's power to take us through.

No matter what you've gone through or are going through, there's a purpose and a plan for your life.

CHAPTER THREE

Principle

Discipline vs. regret

Finding Purpose:
Understanding the Will of God

In the years preceding my decision to re-commit my life to Christ, I was restless and unhappy. I thought that a move would help; therefore, I would often spend time in the mountains or at the beach, but the void never left. It would be years later before I would understand why I lacked fulfillment and a genuine passion for life.

We were designed to fellowship with God, to do His will and to obey His principles. Walking outside of this plan often brings discouragement and disappointment. Searching for purpose affects every area of life. It can determine where we'll live, whom we'll marry, where we'll work and how we'll spend our time. Unfortunately, many search for purpose and meaning in material possessions, hobbies and other things that do not hold eternal value. If you believe that materially successful people are happy, think again. Most of us understand that money can buy the best mattress, but it can't guarantee sleep. Why do millionaires, movie stars and top entertainers often turn to spirituality, drugs and alcohol for the answers if success satisfies? Many discover that money, fame and recognition are not the answers. CEOs, presidents and vice presidents frequently admit that they are happy when they reach production goals, but very unhappy when under budget, *largely because they measure happiness by what's happening to them.* When things go well, they're happy, when things go poorly, they're unhappy. I'm not suggesting that we shouldn't be productive, but if happiness is measured by our circumstances, it's going to be a very rough road.

One of the happiest times in my life, for example, was when I went from running multiple fitness locations to making much less money digging ditches, writing and managing nothing but my daily life. During this transition, I quickly learned that the more I owned, the more owned me.

> *The more I owned, the more owned me.*

Goals, dreams and aspirations are God's desire for our lives, but when these things are based on self-gratification, we encounter problems emotionally, physically and spiritually.

Proverbs 13:12 states, "Hope deferred makes the heart sick, but when the desire comes, it is a tree of life." In other words, when our godly desires are fulfilled, it brings joy to our lives. The goal then is to align our desires with God's. God wants us to experience a fulfilled and abundant life, but we must look to the right source. Abundant life can include material wealth, but it does not depend upon it.

God plants desire in our heart. Without desire, one is not inclined to pursue vocations like medicine, law, professional ministry, education, construction, sales and so on. God wants us to pursue our interests. Again, He is the one who created that desire, but our definition of prosperity often centers on financial prosperity, or what makes us comfortable.

When I worked in the health and fitness industry, many of us wanted to retire at a young age and do nothing but fish and relax on the beach, or by a lake. This sounds nice, but it shouldn't be our goal. God wants us to enjoy these things, but not to make them our primary focus. III John 2 states, "Beloved, I pray that you may prosper in all things and be in health, just as your soul prospers." The statement, *as your soul prospers,* reminds us that spiritual prosperity is first and foremost; it is fundamental to our overall health and sense of well-being. In short, we can't experience true success and fulfillment without first considering the health of our soul.

Prosperity, by most definitions, means *a state of abundance.* A husband may want a large home, expensive toys and a huge bank account, but that's not what his wife needs. She needs to first feel a sense of emotional security, attention, understanding, compassion and a relationship with her husband. Ask most men how they are doing, and they'll immediately tell you about their business, their career or their hobbies. On occasions, I've made this mistake. My pastor, Sean Appleton, brought this to my attention when he restated the question, "No, I mean how is your wife, your family and your relationship with the Lord?"

I often hear men say that it's *quality* not *quantity* that counts when it comes to spending time with family members. Let's apply this thought to other areas of life and test its validity. Does a quality ten-minute workout once a week produce results? Does eating a quality meal once a week lead to better health? Does spending a few quality minutes at work lead to financial success? You can see where this is going . . . both quality and quantity matter. Try this test: invite your wife and kids to honestly share how important *time* is to them; you may be surprised at their answer.

PASSION DRIVEN BY PURPOSE

Our passion and purpose in life should be closely interwoven. Those who have a passion for teaching children, for example, often find joy as a schoolteacher. Problems arise when we seek comfort, convenience, money, status or recognition above the passion that God has placed within us. Literally millions of men are unhappy simply because they chose a lucrative career rather than a career that they were gifted for and enjoy. Let me offer a suggestion, primarily for young men: most colleges offer career testing and counseling, and there may be options you've never considered. You may want to take the opportunity to explore your talents and interests with a professional assessment and guidance counselor, or God may want you right where you are. Either way, He offers timeless principles as we pursue our purpose . . .

➤ He stresses patience—we want it now.

➤ He wants to prepare us—we think we're ready.

➤ He wants to train us—we want to do it our way.

➤ He wants what's best for us—we'll take second best.

➤ He wants to mold us into His image—we're more concerned with self-image.

Again, you can see where this is going. It's all about us, and what we want, but we need to recognize that there is a Master Builder who has a plan.

Lacking passion can be as disheartening as lacking income. The Great Depression of the early 1900's brought devastation through financial ruin. Why then does today's society experience so much unhappiness when we are at the pinnacle of financial success? It's simple . . . passion for life is directly related to purpose in life. *Many are living, but there is no life in their years.* Without God truly directing our lives, life-long fulfillment and purpose is hard to achieve. You might say, "I go to church but still lack passion." Although it helps, going to church doesn't guarantee spiritual fulfillment any more than going to the gym guarantees health. Spiritual fulfillment requires lifestyle changes and focused attention as does maintaining health.

> *Going to church doesn't guarantee spiritual fulfillment any more than going to the gym guarantees health.*

Most of us feel depressed from time to time, simply as a result of our human condition. Physical conditions, adverse circumstances, chemical imbalances, spiritual attacks or combinations can create feelings of despair, dependency and hopelessness. How do you avoid the emotional roller-coaster? First, check the obvious. Who are you associating with? What thoughts fill your mind? Are you walking in obedience to God's Word? Are you spending time in prayer and reading the Bible? If you are doing all you know to do, and nothing seems to help, you may need professional advice. Mild depression and sadness are common to all of us, but when it lingers, it often requires more focused attention. Exercise, fun, friendship, forgiveness, kindness—all are natural chemical enhancers and can gradually help with recovery, but again, there are clear cases of clinical depression that require professional assistance.

Fulfilling our purpose in life is not a destination; it's a journey through day-to-day opportunities. It can be filled with unforeseen and uncharted territory, but it's a rewarding journey if you're looking to the Creator to provide the compass. *True fulfillment comes from having a God-given purpose for your life, and then acting on that purpose.* (Pastor Rick Warren has written an exceptional book entitled, *The Purpose Driven Life* that I highly recommend.)

In the March/April 2003 edition of *New Man* magazine, Pastor Rick Warren told editor Robert Andrescik, "It's not about finding the right career, achieving your dreams or planning your life or reducing your schedule. It's really about, 'Why did God put you here?' and you can only get that by going directly to the Bible." Warren added that the reason many men are insecure is because they lack identity and purpose. . . . "You know, they [men] look for answers in pornography and illicit relationships and stuff like that because they don't know their identity, they don't know their purpose. So they're trying to fill a hole that was never meant to be filled by sex or even success for that matter." I couldn't agree more. Many do not have a true vision for their life. They buy and

They buy and build, invest and earn, date and marry, but are still unfulfilled.

If you don't know where you're going you'll probably get there.

build, invest and earn, date and marry, but are still unfulfilled. Without a vision, their journey becomes mindless wandering. It's been said . . . if you don't know where you're going you'll probably get there. Vision brings hope and direction. The Bible affirms, "Where there is no vision, the people perish . . ." (Proverbs 29:18 KJV). Therefore, in order to find true peace, fulfillment and contentment, we must ask God for purpose and vision. Pride will sidetrack us with thoughts such as, "I know what's best and I'll do what I want." Satan lost his position in heaven because of pride, and Eve sampled the fruit not only because it looked good, but because she was enticed by the idea of being like God; therefore, the first step in finding your purpose in life is to . . .

1. **Remove the detour of pride.** Seeking direction and admitting that we need God's help, is the first step in receiving direction. Jesus often healed the blind, but only when they asked for vision. You might begin by praying, "Lord, I've been pursuing my own will. I'm asking You to direct me in all areas of life, and to reveal my gifts and to use those gifts to help others. You created me, and I want You to direct me. Open my eyes so that I might see."

2. The next step is to **align your will with His.** This is often the hardest step to take. It may require moving, changing careers, ending certain relationships or making other lifestyle changes, but it begins with daily Bible reading, prayer and godly counsel. During this process, God often lightens the load and/or redirects our path. Hebrews 12:1 (NLT) states, ". . . let us strip off every weight that slows us down, especially the sin that so easily hinders our progress. And let us run with endurance the race that God has set before us."

3. The next step is to **stay focused on the goal.** The following verse in Hebrews reads, "We do this by keeping our eyes on Jesus, on whom our faith depends from start to finish . . ." (Hebrews 12:2). Many, no doubt, ask God for direction, but as soon as challenges arise, they give up and return to their comfort zone. We may easily jump ship unless we realize that God's will often does not relieve

us of challenges, rather it reveals our motives. Our job is to keep our eyes continually on Christ, regardless of challenges.

> *God's will often does not relieve us of challenges, rather it reveals our motives.*

The good news is that regardless of what you have done up to this point, you can once again position yourself in the center of God's will. Again, God's will and your purpose in life were intended to go hand-in-hand. With God's direction, life-long fulfillment and purpose are inevitable.

KNOWING THE WILL OF GOD

There are far greater books written on knowing the will of God than what I can express in a few short pages. Authors such as Jack Hayford, Charles Stanley, Josh McDowell, James Dobson, and Chuck Swindoll, to name only a few, have written exceptional books on the subject.

The following pages will not outline God's specific will for your life; however, they will outline certain principles and truths that provide guidance for the journey.

Knowing the will of God is a desire we all have, but unfortunately, many focus on the external circumstances of life and not on the inner condition of the heart. We may live in a certain location, have the job we want and be married to the person of our choice, but often, many of our plans don't produce the peace or fulfillment that we had hoped for, largely because

> *Many focus on the external circumstances of life and not on the inner condition of the heart.*

we don't align our will with God's. *We want what we think will make us happy—God wants to develop our character* and prepare us for an eternal reward. Although topics such as marriage and career are important to address, they don't supercede our need to address character development. For instance, God's will for my life is centered less on the *What Works Book Series* and more on who I am as a person, both in private and in public. *Reputation is who we are around others; character is who we are when no one is around.* It's been said that you can tell cowards from heroes by which way they run. In the same way, character is the most powerful tool in transmitting to others who we are and what we stand for. America has some of the most talented athletes, entrepreneurs and businessmen in the world, but ability will only take them as far as their character will allow them to go. They may climb the ladder of success, but it's their character that will keep them at the top. Corporate America definitely offers rich opportunity, and without profit, companies cease to exist, but they need to be character-driven as well as production-driven. Lately, we have witnessed the downfall of corporations that lost the balance between profitability and accountability. Character traits such as integrity, honesty, loyalty and trust were somehow removed from company policy.

> *Ability will only take you as far as your character will allow you to go.*

It takes time to develop godly character; don't get discouraged. Although good character is a matter of choice, it is also forged through affliction and tempered by adversity; it is built through the challenges we face and the obstacles we overcome.

Godly character can rebuild a marriage, restore a relationship and influence others to follow its lead. In contrast, bad character can ruin a marriage, destroy a relationship and draw the wrong crowd. Words, choices and habits all reflect character. Therefore, the first step in seeking God's will is to continually develop godly character and to allow Him to direct your steps—"The steps of a good man are ordered by the Lord . . ." (Psalm 37:23).

After you make a commitment to develop godly character, *focus on making a difference not a dollar.* Those who are the most fulfilled are often those who focus on making a difference in the lives of others. Focusing primarily on personal needs is a never-ending pull that satisfies only momentarily. I want to stress this point because this is where we continually fall. Proverbs 1:19 offers . . . "Such is the fate of all who are greedy for gain. It ends up robbing them of life" (NLT). To be robbed of life means to be robbed of joy, peace and contentment. Ironically, *self-centeredness takes from oneself rather than gives; it robs from life.* When we primarily seek personal gain, it affects every area of life, especially marriage.

In retrospect of my early years in the fitness industry, I found that when I focused on earning a large paycheck, I wasn't fulfilled; however, when I focused on helping others, I was fulfilled. You've heard it said, and I quickly learned, that people don't care how much you know until they know how much you care—kindness can be more impressive than a paycheck, and it's more fulfilling. Focus on making a positive difference in the lives of others; you'll never regret that decision.

The Bible often illustrates the fact that God is working on character rather than on superficial things. In the Old Testament, for example, God gave many men the opportunity to be leaders, and it was character, not position, that determined their outcome.

> *It was character, not position, that determined their outcome.*

When we are walking in obedience to God's Word, many times, the struggles that we encounter are not an indicator that we are out of God's will but rather that He is molding us into His image, or they are part of a plan. Mary and Joseph could easily have questioned God's will when Mary, pregnant and ready to deliver, rode on a donkey to an unfamiliar town only to find that there was no room for her to lodge and to give birth.

Instead of asking, "What is God's will for my life?" We should be asking, "How can I develop and strengthen my character while pursuing His will?" Once we give our lives to Christ and seek His direction, we can often sense His lead, but if we're actively engaging in sin, His direction will be hard to distinguish, if at all. It's been well stated . . . hearing God's voice can keep us from sin, or sin can keep us from hearing God's voice. The Scripture, ". . . A life of moral excellence leads to knowing God

> *Hearing God's voice can keep us from sin, or sin can keep us from hearing God's voice.*

better" (II Peter 1:5 NLT), assures us that one of the best ways to know God's plans are to live life morally upright.

As you pursue your purpose, let me offer two closing points that have helped me stay focused in the "right" direction. First, *pursue the desire that God has placed in your heart.* Although many people encouraged me to start a construction company or pursue a degree when I left the fitness industry, I knew that God had different plans, and I pursued those plans regardless of what others suggested. This does not mean that we shouldn't seek counsel, but when it comes to pursuing your dreams, others may not share your vision. (A degree from the Master is far more valuable than a Master's Degree.)

Second, *continually check your reasons for pursuing your goals.* If you're pursuing dreams solely for financial gain or prideful reasons, you're on the wrong path. God clearly blesses and provides but our motives must stem from a pure heart.

How well do you hear?

Many times, we have the order reversed; we want to hear from God and then we'll work on our character. God tells us to work on character and then we'll be better able to hear. Here are some keys to hear correctly . . .

➢ **Recognize that God's will is not as clearly defined as a road map.** "Should I turn left or right?" "Should I work, read or exercise?" "Should I sleep in or get up?" The *"should I's"* can be endless. God's will is a journey as well as a destination. God told Abraham in Genesis 12:1, ". . . go to the land that I will show you" (NLT). So it is with us. He teaches us to sense His direction through the guidance of the Holy Spirit, and to move accordingly. Sometimes we do experience a true sense of God's exact direction, but often, we simply walk by faith. If you feel that God is leading you and if the leading does not run contrary to His Word, move forward even if it seems unclear at times. Generally, it's simply a matter of acknowledging Proverbs 3:6 . . . commit your ways to Him daily, trusting that He is directing your path (paraphrased).

> *God's will is a journey as well as a destination.*

➤ **Compare what you're feeling to the Word of God.** How often do
we sense a stirring in our spirit and are not sure if it's God or not,
especially when making important decisions? A good question to
ask is, "Am I following my flesh or God?" Remember, God's will
always corresponds with His Word. For example, if an opportunity
arises to increase your income through dishonest gain, the decision
is easy: pass on the so-called "opportunity." Contrary to God's
Word, many Christians date and marry unbelievers. Regardless of
feelings, God's Word does not change. Does this mean that God
cannot bless Christians if they've married unbelievers? No, but
*being equally yoked is not just a good idea; it is God's principle
intended to promote the health of the relationship.* The more we
ignore God's leading, the harder it becomes to hear His voice; we
can become spiritually deaf. Again, compare your direction to
Scripture. Does it line up? Step away and take time to analyze.
Again, you can't go wrong by waiting for direction, but you can
often go wrong rushing.

➤ **Accept the assignment.** This is difficult for me because I like
telling God what to do. For example, when I felt the
overwhelming sense to sell my home, I knew that God was
leading me away from Corporate America and into the unknown,
but I fought the urge to sell. I thought, "Surely God will allow
me to keep my home," but eventually I put it on the market. I
hoped that it wouldn't sell, but it did; within three weeks I had
an offer. At the last minute I backed out, still believing that God
wanted me to own a custom home. During the months that
followed, the desire to leave my career was greater than ever, and
I knew that I needed to sell my house. In a rush, I contacted a
real-estate agent and sold it within a few months. However, I
received thousands of dollars less than I would have received
initially had I listened and heeded His voice. When we hear from
God, we need to respond in faith. God is not playing games like
"Do this," "No, I mean do that," "No, do this again." The key is
to heed the *correct* voice, use wisdom and move forward. I felt
that it was the correct leading because it was the wise thing to
do—I needed to save money more than I needed a new home.
Was it easy at first? Hardly, but the weeks that followed brought
tremendous comfort.

> **Patiently and quietly listen.** You can hear the still, small voice of the Holy Spirit by spending time in prayer and learning from God's Word. If you've ever sat quietly outside your home in the calm of the morning, you've probably noticed many of the sounds that you do not hear throughout the day. Those sounds generally continue throughout the day, but as the day progresses, they are overcome by the sounds of our busy lives. In order to hear, it's necessary to remove oneself from the activity of the day. When God spoke to Elijah in 1 Kings 19:11-12, the Scriptures state that the wind and the fire came, and that the storms thundered, but that God was not in them; He was, however, in the still, small voice that followed (paraphrased). God wants our undivided attention each and every day. Without a shadow of doubt, moving too quickly can have major consequences. We often want answers and we want them now. It's difficult to patiently wait. Patience may be compared to a control valve used to help us avoid making decisions based on emotional response. Much like a control device used for a dam to release water, if the valve is broken, water levels rise and can overflow, causing destruction below. In the same way, if we don't allow patience to control our decisions, they may ultimately cause damage. One can never go wrong by saying, "God, I believe that I moved too fast and haven't been patient in this area, I want to take time and focus on You. I trust that You will lead me and show me what to do." If you feel rushed, simply step back and re-evaluate the situation. Stepping back doesn't mean giving up; it means patiently seeking God's direction as you move forward. When we are impatient, we can easily become confused; confusion often leads to emotional, unsound decisions. We may say and do things that jeopardize our marriage, our careers and our relationships. I Corinthians 14:33 states, "For God is not the author of confusion but of peace. . . ." Patience allows us time to see things for what they really are, and to see others in a variety of situations and under a variety of conditions. Waiting provides opportunity to determine if the decision we're about to make is the right one, or a *rushed* one. When I first felt the need to sell my home, I prayed about it and patiently waited. My desire to sell continued to grow and many godly people confirmed the decision because it was the wise thing to do. Many of us lead very busy lives, which makes it difficult to

be in the right frame of mind to hear from God. It wasn't until I spent each morning in solitude and prayer that I began to sense direction. As I read, and prayed, and fasted occasionally, His will began to unfold. I cannot stress enough the importance of setting aside time each day to seek God's will for your life. If you're too busy to do this, you may be too busy, and may be missing an opportunity for more productive time and time management. From my experience, I found that God doesn't always say yes or no immediately, He tells us to wait and be patient. His leading isn't a thoughtless course of action; it's a well-designed plan that requires patience, and patience builds character. On another note, it's incredibly difficult to hear God if we're actively engaging in sin. Sin means *to miss the mark*—we can't be on target, in the center of God's will, if we're always missing the mark.

➤ **Keep moving.** You might ask, "If we are to patiently wait and quietly listen, how can we keep moving?" Although there are clearly times when God wants us to wait, it's difficult to direct what's not moving. During my childhood and teen years, my family often vacationed and fished in the Eastern Sierra Nevada Mountain Range near June Lake, California. Once on the lake, Dad would accelerate the boat motor and head off until we reached our destination. He would then shut off the motor and lower the anchor. On one occasion (when I was very young), after the motor was stilled and we began fishing, I tried steering the boat. No matter which direction I turned the wheel, the boat stood still. I asked my dad why the boat wasn't working. He said that it was working but that it could not be directed unless it was moving. In the same way, God may be directing us, but if we're not moving, we won't get anywhere. Moving doesn't mean walking around without an agenda, it means serving God and others, living life to the fullest and doing our best each and every day. I repeatedly tell singles . . . *God often brings a spouse when they're moving in the right direction, not looking in the wrong direction.* This is often referred to as "waiting on the Lord." Like a waiter in a restaurant, waiting often means serving God and others. Isaiah 40:31 concludes, "But they that wait upon the Lord shall renew their strength; they shall mount up with wings as eagles; they shall run, and not be weary; and they shall walk, and not faint" (KJV).

➤ **His will is often revealed over time.** Most of us want immediate answers when we seek direction, but more often than not, if it's not written, *God's will tends to be a process rather than an instant revelation.* Granted, there are times when the Holy Spirit directs us instantly—prompting a phone call to a friend in need, or leading us to make a quick decision, but we usually see only portions of the big picture. When I felt an inner sense directing me to leave an eight-year profession, I only saw glimpses of the big picture. It seemed unlikely, but I envisioned myself writing books, speaking and promoting Christian values. I had no idea how it would unfold, but God asks us to walk in faith and trust Him.

➤ **Don't be surprised by challenges.** I once believed that life was easy while in the center of God's will and if life wasn't easy, I was out of His will. This is not always true. Yes, we should have peace in the center of God's will, but at times we may fight bouts of anxiety, depression and fear. Many in the Bible fought hardship and anxiety while being in the center of God's will. Abraham, Sarah, Joseph, Moses, Elijah, Esther, Jeremiah, Isaiah, Mary, the Apostle Paul, the Disciples, all faced difficult times and challenging circumstances. When I finished writing *What Works When "Diets" Don't*, for example, I experienced periods of anxiety and depression. Was this an indicator that I was out of God's will? Of course not—His will was in process. I trusted Him, kept moving forward and continued working toward my goals. Was it easy? No, but within a few months, new opportunities arose. How can we determine if we are in God's will, even when challenges arise? First, focus on God's moral will for your life and demonstrate honesty and integrity when making decisions. Second, focus on obeying His principles such as helping others, tithing, reading the Bible, praying, and so on. Third, seek counsel, use wisdom and rely on God to guide you. Is it trouble-free? Not at all. Unquestionably, being in the center of

God's will does not prevent challenges; sometimes it creates them, but as long as you are following His direction, walking morally upright and obeying His principles, rest assured that He will direct you—one way or the other.

➢ **God's will is always what's best for you.** I remember, as a teen, feeling that when I committed my life to Christ all the fun would be over. You probably know people who feel this way—maybe that's you. Nothing could be farther from the truth; God's will is always what is best for you although it may not feel like it from time to time. He's placed godly desires within you, and those desires will manifest themselves as you pursue His will. Missionaries will often tell you that they had a deep desire to serve God as a missionary. Many Christian businessmen and professionals also say they too felt inclined toward their specific field. God does not give talent and interests to be wasted; He encourages the desires of your heart as you seek to serve Him and others—God is the one who places the desire within you. (If you truly lack motivation and energy, consider taking a closer look at your overall health.)

➢ **His leading is generally calm and reassuring.** On a closing note, God seldom rushes us. Although there may be times when we must make a quick, timely decision, His will is generally calm and reassuring. If you feel rushed, stop and wait. If, for some reason, you can't wait, simply use wisdom and make the decision to the best of your ability. If you are seeking a spouse, a home, a job, or other things, slow down, position yourself in God's will and wait on Him. You can rarely go wrong waiting, but you can often go wrong rushing.

> *You can rarely go wrong waiting, but you can often go wrong rushing.*

THE PAIN OF DISCIPLINE VS. THE PAIN OF REGRET

In closing, from time to time, you may feel helpless and depressed even when you're doing all that you know to do. You may even lose confidence in your ability, and feel like giving up and returning to your familiar comfort zone. DON'T! This thinking is wrong! Press through. You are exercising the very important muscle of perseverance. There is a saying that ships are safest in the harbor, but they are not made for the harbor (William Shedd). Likewise, you were designed to weather storms successfully. *When life becomes difficult and challenging, set your sites on the goal not on the challenge.* You were not created to fail, you were created to succeed—and make sure you remember the true meaning of "success." There is a blessing just beyond the circumstance. Simply trust that God is leading despite appearances and keep moving forward.

> *Ships are safest in the harbor, but they are not made for the harbor.*

Finding your purpose in life while pursuing the will of God definitely requires discipline. Discipline is one of the most important character qualities we possess. Ironically, those things we generally like to do such as viewing television, playing video games, sleeping or surfing the Internet are easy, but activities such as working, praying, reading the Bible, serving and spending quality time with family, seem to be the most difficult. That's why discipline is vitally important; it helps us do what we don't *feel* like doing, but later leaves us deeply satisfied and glad that we did.

Discipline is simply putting our choice into action. If we exercise discipline in one area, it will help to regulate and strengthen this control valve in other areas. For instance, those who regularly practice the discipline of exercising, often find that other areas of life improve. The principle of discipline cannot be overlooked when it comes to succeeding in any area of life, whether

> *Discipline is simply putting our choice into action.*

financially, relationally or spiritually. Be leery of those who say that discipline or willpower isn't important. Discipline is not only important to success—it's essential!

Are you working hard toward your goals, and are you working smart? Is what you're doing producing the results you want? If not, reconsider what you're doing and simply make another choice. Above all, make the change while you still have the choice and remember that the ability to "stick to it" is what separates those who succeed from those who almost succeed. You possess tremendous inner power and strength. You've been given the power to make decisions, the power to develop habits and the power to choose at any given time. Many are willing to break a habit, lose weight, improve a marriage, attend church or seek God more fervently, but willingness alone is not enough. Willingness must be followed by action, and action, in this sense, is simply discipline in motion.

> *The ability to "stick to it" is what separates those who succeed from those who almost succeed.*

Forget past failures; instead decide what you're going to do with the days, weeks, months and years ahead. Don't live with ongoing regret. Take control of your life and change your direction. *Don't look back unless it's the direction you want to go.* You can't change where you've been, but you can change where you're going. The Apostle Paul stresses, ". . . but one thing I do, forgetting those things which are behind and reaching forward to those things which are ahead" (Philippians 3:13). It can be easier to prepare for physical exertion than to prepare for the mental exertion of life: use the calmer times to prepare for the challenges ahead, not only physically, but also mentally; read, rest and practice patience in the little things. Much like an athlete who prepares all year for the one-day event, he or she doesn't win the event in one day; it is a gradual practice of preparation, discipline and perseverance. Little disciplines, practiced day-by-day, produce winning results.

Our thoughts become words, our words actions and our actions become habits.

(Paraphrased motto of the Metropolitan Milwaukee YMCA.)

CHAPTER FOUR

Principle

Preparation

The Source of Our Strength Comes from the Food We Choose

There was a young man who was determined to find help for his troubled life. After years of frustration and regret, he was deeply discouraged and despondent. He had worked several years and had nothing to show for it. He had been easily influenced, and most of his friends were major contributors to his negative attitude. As a result, his mind was constantly filled with depressing thoughts.

The young man was determined to find help. He walked to a neighboring church and found a pastor at work in his study. He told the pastor that he was a Christian but that he had a difficult life. He wanted to make better choices, but he couldn't seem to stay on track.

The young man continued, "It's as if I have two dogs constantly battling within me. One dog is evil and negative, while the other is good and positive!" He continued to say that the battles were long and very difficult; they drained him emotionally and mentally to the point of exhaustion. He explained further that he couldn't seem to make the right choices in life.

Without a moment's thought, the pastor asked the young man, "Which dog wins the battle?" Looking a bit confused, the young man said, "The constant battle leaves me depressed and feeling negative, and I often look for something to kill the pain. Isn't it obvious that the evil dog wins?" The pastor looked at the young man and wisely said, "Then that's the dog you feed the most! *If you want to experience victory, you need to starve that dog to death!*"

He realized, as should we, that *the source of our strength comes from the food we choose*—what we feed grows, and what grows becomes the dominating force within our lives. In order to win the battle in our mind, we need more of Christ and less of the world living within us. One or the other will prevail but it's up to us how much we allow in. If we attend church sporadically, open the Bible on holidays and pray only when we are in need, it will not be enough to overcome the constant bombardment of outside influence. Again, it's our choice!

> *What we feed grows, and what grows becomes the dominating force within our lives.*

YOU CAN ENTER OR EXIT

Preparation is a key ingredient to success; without it, destiny is left to chance. Armies that are undefeated are well prepared. Companies that survive fluctuating economies are prepared. Successful marriages are prepared. Preparation simply means to be ready for the challenges ahead. Olympic athletes spend years preparing for one event. In the same way, we should spend time preparing for the unforeseen challenges ahead. Remember, we play like we practice.

I once misunderstood those who chose not to watch certain movies and television programs, attend certain events or listen to suggestive music; they were, in my eyes, fanatical. I now realize that *if I don't control my desires, my desires will control me—right thinking creates right doing!* For instance, after I recommitted my life to Christ, my cravings for alcohol seemed to increase at times. A week or two would go by and eventually the desire to drink again resurfaced. As I continued to analyze my situation, I noticed that every time I watched certain television programs, listened to most secular music or associated with the wrong crowd (a major snare), the desire to drink would increase. I quickly learned the truth in: what we feed grows and what grows becomes the controlling force within our lives.

If we want to experience spiritual victory, we must choose our food wisely. We'll never be completely free from wrong desires; there is a constant struggle to resist temptation, but there's a clear difference between a struggle and a lifestyle. Even Christ was tempted, but he was not drawn away by sin.

One way we can escape certain temptations is to make the necessary lifestyle changes. As I was concluding this chapter, three men that I knew shared with me that they were trying to overcome strongholds in their lives. One was addicted to alcohol, the others to drugs.

In each case, I was intrigued by the similarities that preceded their abuse. Each vowed never to use again, and I'm confident that they truly meant it. Within a week or two, however, they would be using or drinking again. They each had said, "I don't know what else to do, I sometimes pray and I go to church when I can." Although all of them prayed from time to time, or went to church on occasion, their *overall* lifestyle did not change; they continued to embrace old habits and make wrong choices. Much like the man who walked into a bar and prayed, "God, please help me not to drink again."

> *Although prayer and attending church are very important, more "right" choices need to be made—a lot more.*

Change requires just that: *change*—don't willingly walk into the enemy's camp. I don't mean to disregard the deep emotional and psychological challenges that accompany addiction; I've experienced them myself, but I do want to remind you that God makes provision for all of our needs, but we must take action on what we know to be right. James 1:21 proclaims, "So get rid of all the filth and evil in your lives, and humbly accept the message God has planted in your hearts, for it is strong enough to save your souls" (NLT). If the Word of God is strong enough to save our souls, how much more can it deliver us from addiction and/or wrong desires?

In their lives, and in my own personal struggle with alcohol, I noticed a common trend, although prayer and attending church are very important, more "right" choices need to be made—a lot more. Our lives must be totally surrendered to Christ. For me, it all came down to this simple statement: *how badly did I want it?* Did I want it enough to . . .

➢ Make my relationship with Christ a *daily* priority?

➢ *Regularly* attend church, pray and read the Bible?

➢ *End* relationships that were pulling me down?

➢ *Avoid* places that triggered wrong desires?

➢ *Enlist* an accountability partner such as a pastor, or a church leader?

➢ Make *all* the necessary lifestyle changes?

This list may seem extreme, but we are in a spiritual battle and preparation is the key to our victory. If something in our life is causing us to stumble, we must remove it (Mark 9:43).

Just for a moment, picture yourself as a soldier being deployed into enemy territory. Just before you land on foreign soil the soldier next to you says, "My gear, guns, and ammo are too heavy, I'm going to fight without it. How about you?" What would you do? What would you say? He has a point; the equipment is heavy and excessive, right? Wrong, it's essential for survival! The enemy's goal is to steal, to kill and to destroy what he can; therefore, you must be prepared. Why then do we often leap into spiritual battle unprepared, unarmed and untrained? Why do we avoid committing our lives to Christ wholeheartedly? The reason it's difficult for men to read the Bible, pray and attend church is because the enemy knows that the Word of God has power over sin and bondage, and he does what he can to lead us astray, or keep us at bay.

Think about it . . . to earn a living we need to continually work and labor. To lose weight and keep it off we need to continually make certain lifestyle changes. To build lasting relationships we must continue to invest in them. In the same way, to defeat the enemy, we must continually commit our lives to Christ and make the necessary changes. *We don't overcome addiction; Christ living within us overcomes the addiction.*

I've also learned that overcoming strongholds takes time; don't become discouraged. Programs like *Alcoholics Anonymous* and treatment centers, for instance, are wonderful tools, but I believe that a relationship with Jesus Christ must be the primary focus. God will not allow you, or I, to be tempted beyond what we are able to withstand. 1 Corinthians 10:13 states, ". . . God is faithful, who will not allow you to be tempted beyond what you are able, but with the temptation will also make the way of escape, that you may be able to bear it." The door of temptation swings both ways—you can enter or exit. That's why we need to be very selective in what we watch and listen to, and how we spend our time. Why would we willingly walk into the enemy's camp? Why would we feed wrong desires and thoughts? Feeding the flesh does nothing but bring war

> *The door of temptation swings both ways—you can enter or exit.*

against the spirit. What we think provides the framework for who we become. Our thoughts become words, our words actions, our actions habits and our habits form our character.

"For we are not fighting against people made of flesh and blood, but against the evil rulers and authorities of the unseen world, against those mighty powers of darkness who rule this world, and against wicked spirits in the heavenly realms" (Ephesians 6:12 NLT). Just because the choice is made to become a Christian, does not mean that life is easy. There is a constant battle within our minds. Galatians 5:17 (NLT) also presents this fact: ". . . the Spirit gives us desires that are opposite from what the sinful nature desires. These two forces are constantly fighting each other, and your choices are never free from this conflict." In other words, our sinful nature and our nature in Christ are constantly at war. Make no mistake about it; our greatest battle is within and preparation is the key to our victory. For example, I believe that a majority of marriages are failing because men are not preparing spiritually for the battles ahead. In many cases, the actions of the husband determine the stability of the marriage. If a company fails, the president is held responsible. If a sports team fails, the coach is held responsible. If a marriage fails, the husband should examine himself. Granted, there are some men who, through no fault of their own, experience a failed marriage or challenging relationship, but for the large majority, there is a critical need for change in attitude and actions. Often, it is the wife who encourages Bible study, church attendance, or prayer, while men willingly forsake their God-intended role for spiritual leadership. There is no greater investment than investing in your spiritual growth and the spiritual safety of your family.

> *In many cases, the actions of the husband determine the stability of the marriage.*

As a word of encouragement, if you feel discouraged, don't be! You can get back on track and change your life today. Often, you'll have two choices: to fall backward or to fall forward. If you choose to fall forward into God's forgiveness, in time God's grace will heal and restore you. Although there are negative consequences for poor choices, there are also positive consequences for wise choices. For instance, according to *The Book of Romance*, only 1 out of 1,050 marriages in which the husband and wife choose to read their Bible together, end in divorce.

> *Only 1 out of 1,050 marriages in which the husband and wife choose to read their Bible together, end in divorce.*

When confronted by sin, God wants us to run to Him, not away. Which way will you run?

THE TOP THREE THINGS TO AVOID

You were created for a reason. Your life has purpose. Again, no matter what you've gone through or are going through, there's a purpose and a destiny for your life, however, the enemy uses three methods to abort our success. Speaking from personal experience and observation, many men sabotage success and their ability to regain lost ground through these three destructive forces. According to 1 John 2:16 (paraphrased), they are . . . the *lust of the flesh* (what we crave), the *lust of the eyes* (what is pleasing to the eye) and the *pride of life* (arrogance).

1. **The lust of the flesh.** Lust can be defined as desire over the boundary lines. All of us struggle with lust in some form or another, the question is do we entertain the thought until it fuels desire and brings forth sin, or do we walk away? Desire is not wrong, but what we do with it can be. If our hearts are sincere and teachable, God can bless us, but if we purposely engage in sin, we remove His protection. Being tempted isn't sin— surrendering to it is. God is merciful to forgive and bestow blessings as we repent and make necessary lifestyle changes. Feelings of lust can be overcome when we read His Word, protect our eyes and ears, educate ourselves, apply wisdom and surround ourselves with those who lift us up rather than pull us down. Addiction, as previously discussed, can also be classified with *the lust of the flesh.* Addiction often means to give oneself up to a habit and then become dependent upon that habit. There are many forms of addiction, from drugs and alcohol, to pornography and work or work related success. Workaholics, for example, can appear as hard working and industrious, but the addiction eventually robs from other relationships, and the spiritual and emotional health of the family is neglected. Many men in America will accept difficult employees, face challenging situations on the job, work exhausting hours, commit fully to the cause of the company and do whatever it takes to get the job done, yet, unfortunately, severely neglect a marriage—*sometimes it appears as if they'd rather lose a wife than a career.* Unfortunately, many may never fully understand or recognize the severity of their problem until the damage is done.

Another downfall, from time to time, is unstable emotions, especially in regard to anger. Scripture addresses anger and our attitude toward it. Ephesians 4:31 declares, "Let all bitterness, wrath, anger, clamor, and evil speaking be put away from you. . . ." Paul understood that in order for a Christian to be effective, anger would have to find its place. Proverbs 14:17 states that "A quick-tempered man acts foolishly. . . ." You may have heard the saying: *don't react instead respond.* Simply put, think before you act, and speak. A reaction often calls for an apology, while a response generally thinks things through and no apologies are needed. Ephesians 4:26-27 says, "Be angry, and do not sin: do not let the sun go down on your wrath, nor give place to the devil." Anger over issues like abortion, pornography, homosexuality, and adultery is justifiable and can evoke a response with positive action. If anger causes damage to another, or personally damages character, it is not accomplishing God's purpose. If anger sparks prayer and a Christ-like stance, it's productive. James 1:20 concludes, "For the wrath of man does not produce the righteousness of God." We'll rarely settle an argument, or win a dispute with anger. We are encouraged to weigh our actions carefully and respond accordingly. Granted this is easier said than done, but it can be done with a continual reliance on God. Many men bring anger into the marriage. As a result, wives become targets and relationships suffer. For many years, I had a difficult time controlling my temper, and at times, it's still a challenge. I have learned that anger cannot be harnessed on its own, only the transforming Word of God and a personal relationship with Christ along with the conviction of the Holy Spirit brings life-long healing. It sounds redundant, but it's true . . . *a daily relationship with Christ through prayer and Scripture reading can eventually calm an angry spirit.* Romans 8:6 NLT states, "If your sinful nature controls your mind, there is death. But if the Holy Spirit controls your mind, there is life and peace." With God's help, you'll begin to control your emotions instead of allowing your emotions to control you, and *nothing feels as good as being in control.*

2. Briefly, **the lust of the eyes** can be defined as coveting, or desiring something such as a trophy wife, expensive home, vehicle or other things. *When we fall prey to lust our focus often*

shifts from Christ-centered to self-centered. The next time a decision needs to be made, try asking . . . "Will this decision please God?" In Matthew 4:8-9 Jesus was also tempted by the lust of the eyes. It states, ". . . the devil took Him to a very high mountain and showed Him all the kingdoms of the world and their glory; and he said to Him, 'All these things I will give You, if You fall down and worship me'" (NASB). Jesus rejected his proposal and defeated him with the Word of God, saying: ". . . For it is written, 'You shall worship the Lord your God, and serve Him only'" (Matthew 4:10 NASB). In the same way, we have the Word of God available to us. Don't become frustrated—change takes time. The process requires patience, consistency and obedience in doing what is right.

3. **The pride of life** is the opposite of humility. It can be defined as conceit, or a sense of superiority in who we are or what we posses. Proverbs 6:16-17 says that *the Lord hates a proud look.* Self-centeredness is closely related to pride. When we believe that our needs are more important than the needs of others, and we think more highly of ourselves than we should, pride is a problem and it will severely hinder our progress. "Pride of life" causes us to place more emphasis on things than on people. A friend of mine, Pastor James Majeske, once delivered a powerful message on pride. He stated, "Pride is the only disease known to man that makes everybody sick except the person who has it." He added, "Humility is not thinking less of yourself, but rather not thinking of yourself at all." A

> *God intended that we love people and use things; instead we tend to love things and use people.*

popular saying bears consideration—God intended that we love people and use things; instead we tend to love things and use people. Pride causes us to take pleasure in the things of the world rather than the things of God. Husbands and wives don't marry filled with love and passion one day only to lose it the next. Marriage slowly deteriorates through more attention to self than spouse. Most who are divorced will say that their marriage was

| A *happy wife can* *mean a happy life.* | initially good, but with time, one or both stopped loving—largely because of selfishness. On the lighter side, it may seem simple and understated, however a happy wife can mean a happy life—a happy wife |

is the result of a husband who is committed to the health of the relationship and who puts her needs above his. Selfishness, simply stated, reflects a silent statement that there is no need for God. It can also lead a wife to feel that she is a liability rather than an asset. A selfish person relies on self-dependence rather than dependence on God, and is proud of it—get rid of it! Self-centeredness leaves little room for other's needs; it stifles spiritual growth and a teachable spirit. Without humility and a teachable spirit, relationships cannot fully develop. When our needs are more important than the needs of others, especially those of a spouse, it can severely damage a relationship. Although difficult at times, it's much easier to walk in humility than it is to stumble through life selfishly. I encourage you to build your life on godly rather than worldly wisdom. If your eyes are fixed on what the world has to offer rather than on what God has to give, an entire lifetime can be wasted.

Let me leave you with this question . . . *if the enemy goes to and fro like a roaring lion seeking whom he may devour* (1 Peter 5:8), *and the eyes of the Lord run to and fro throughout the whole earth, to show Himself strong on behalf of those whose heart is loyal to Him* (II Chronicles 16:9); who finds you—the adversary, or God?" Are you loyal to God by obeying His Word, or do you often stray from the Shepherd and become easy prey? Don't let this discourage you: ". . . greater is He who is in you than he who is in the world" (1 John 4:4 NASB). The key is to maintain your loyalty to Christ. Additionally, Paul advises us in Philippians 4:8 (NLT) to ". . . Fix your thoughts on what is true and honorable and right. Think about things that are pure and lovely and admirable. Think about things that are excellent and worthy of praise." Additionally, he states, "For though we walk in the flesh, we do not war according to the flesh. For the weapons of our warfare are not carnal but mighty in God for pulling down strongholds, casting down arguments and every high thing that exalts itself against the knowledge of God, *bringing every thought into captivity to the obedience of Christ*" (II Corinthians 10:3-5—italics mine). Paul understood, as should we, that good thoughts will eventually produce good actions.

> *Good thoughts will eventually produce good actions.*

In Matthew 7:25, Jesus states "and the rain descended, the floods came, and the winds blew and beat on that house; and it did not fall, for it was founded on the rock." The wise man, the man who built his house on the solid rock of Christ rather than on the shifting sand of man's philosophy, withstood the storm, but the foolish man who did not build his house on solid ground lost everything (Matthew 7:27). Strive to build character rich in patience, trust, love, perseverance, commitment and godly wisdom. God will provide plenty of opportunity through experience to develop these qualities; therefore, it's important to see challenges as opportunities for growth. Remember, both men encountered a storm. Adversity comes to all of us. Be prepared and build your life expecting storms (especially in marriage), and maintain a trusting attitude under the direction of the Holy Spirit.

In short, to prepare we must: choose spiritual food wisely, focus on long-term lifestyle changes, make building a relationship with Christ our main priority, avoid feeding lust and selfishness, and prepare in advance. Again, change is a process; don't become frustrated. Be willing to change, willing to learn and willing to use both as stepping-stones to success while continually holding your ground.

PRE-PLANNED MEANS PREPARED:

In your journal, take the time now to plan for success. How are you preparing for change? Will you purchase a good study Bible, choose spiritual food wisely, begin making the necessary lifestyle changes, enlist an accountability partner and avoid places that feed wrong desires? You may want to visit www.familylife.com or www.family.org and review their list of resources, or visit www.whydietsdontwork.com for help with weight-loss and fitness.

JOURNAL EXAMPLE:

Spiritual growth:	6 A.M.—prayer/Bible study/journal
Family:	7 A.M.—time with family
Health & fitness:	8 A.M.—exercise

Begin with a plan. Again, "Where there is no vision, the people perish . . ." (Proverbs 29:18 KJV). A "God-given" vision will bring life to everything you do. Granted, you will need to make adjustments for unexpected events, but get back on track as soon as possible. In 30 days, evaluate again. If not on track, decide how you can prepare for the next 30 days. And remember to *stay focused, and fix your eyes on what lies before you. Mark out a straight path for your feet, and don't get sidetracked; keep your feet from following evil* (Proverbs 4:25-27 NLT).

It's not the fall that hurts—it's staying down that does.

List your short-term and long-term goals and refer to them often. This will help you stay focused. After all, it's not the fall that hurts—it's staying down that does.

The quality of choice today, affects
the quality of life tomorrow.

CHAPTER FIVE

Principle

Wisdom—Choose Wisely

Consider the Results

One way to gauge wisdom, or good judgment, is to consider the results. In Matthew 11:19, the Jewish people were having difficulty grasping the unexpected nature of Jesus' ministry. Many alleged that John the Baptist, the one chosen to prepare the way for Jesus, was demon-possessed and that Jesus was a glutton and drunkard. Instead of arguing with them, Jesus made this statement ". . . But wisdom is shown to be right by what results from it" (NLT). Godly wisdom bears righteous fruit: people received healing and deliverance, and many accepted Christ as their Savior. This was obviously not the work of demons, drunkards or gluttons. Jesus encouraged them to look at the end result and not at how things appeared.

Again, we gauge good judgment by considering the outcome. Do your choices produce the results you want? If not, consider who's leading you—God's Word or the cultural value system and mindset. Does our present society promote good judgment and/or produce good outcomes? Is society building godly leaders and developing admirable character? Let's take a look . . .

All too often . . .

Daily Bible reading and prayer is called "fanatical" while working twelve hours a day is called "success."

Talking, chewing gum and making noise were the top three public school problems in the early sixties. Currently, rape, robbery and assault lead the list.

We build our career and neglect our marriage.

Corporate executives are praised and family men frowned upon.

We protest war but say little about abortion.

We can act out murder, adultery and arson while playing a video game and call it "healthy" entertainment.

We've increased our wealth, but decreased our values.

We take better care of our cars than our bodies.

We search the heavens for answers and turn from the One who created them.

Pride is considered an asset and humility a liability.

We know more about our favorite athletes than our wives and our children.

We'd rather be seen leaving a bar than leaving a church.

Televisions are replaced from over-use while Bibles become dusty.

We raise our hands and praise our favorite team, yet appear handcuffed in church.

We call ourselves a Christian nation; yet reject the biblical principles that made us great.

And we call this progress.

Although we see these attitudes around the world, it is most disheartening to see them in North America because we have known better and have drifted so far from the truth. Granted, it can be discouraging to read facts like these, but don't allow a declining culture to erode essential qualities in your life. You can make a difference and reverse these trends as you follow God's commands, seek direction and pursue the opportunity that He has given you to make a difference. *Be grateful and consider it a privilege that God has chosen you for such a time as this.*

TOO CLOSE TO THE EDGE

Without a doubt, the largest factor contributing to the moral decline of our nation is the lack of sexual purity. Why then do so many continue to fall in this area? I vividly remember a message by Bishop Jakes delivered to a group of prisoners at San Quinton Prison. In regard to repeating destructive behavior, many asked why they chronically found themselves back in prison. Bishop Jakes told the story of a young boy who kept falling out of his bed week after week. The boy finally asked his mother why he kept falling and she wisely answered, "It's because you don't get far enough in!" In the same way, *many of us fall back into sin because we're too close to the edge and we don't move far enough in to God's framework of safety and protection.*

Overcoming sin, especially sexual sin, can be a difficult battle for Christians. On one hand, the Apostle Paul declares, "Our old sinful selves were crucified with Christ so that sin might lose its power in our lives . . ." (Romans 6:6 NLT). Yet, in the next chapter he states, "For the good that I will to do, I do not do; but the evil I will not to do, that I practice" (Romans 7:19). His lament continues in verse twenty-four, "Oh, what a miserable person I am! Who will free me from this life that is dominated by sin?" (NLT). It leaves one to wonder that *if I'm dead to sin why is it still alive in me?* How can Paul declare that he is dead to sin in one verse, yet also ask 'who will free me from the domination of sin in my life?' In addition, Romans 6:16 (NLT) states, ". . . that whatever you choose to obey becomes your master? You can choose sin, which leads to death, or you can choose to obey God and receive His approval." Paul was not saying that he has no power over sin; he was saying that, on his own, he is defenseless. The next verse reads, ". . . Once you were slaves of sin . . ." (6:17 NLT). A slave is one who is owned by another, or dominated by some influence. When Paul says that his life is dominated by sin; he's declaring that life here on earth is strongly influenced by the enemy. Sin is present in this world, but its power over us is crucified when we accept Christ's sacrifice. The question then becomes: do we position ourselves to be drawn away by the strong pull of sin, or do we align ourselves to be firmly footed on solid ground? Isaiah 7:9 instructs, ". . . If you do not stand firm in your faith, you will not stand at all" (NIV). The only way to stand against the enemy is to stand strong in your faith. A half-hearted approach stands on unstable ground. Where are you standing?

Do we position ourselves to be drawn away by the strong pull of sin, or do we align ourselves to be firmly footed on solid ground?

Paul also states, "Do not let sin control the way you live; do not give in to its lustful desires" (Romans 6:12 NLT). As noted earlier, whatever we feed grows, and what grows will largely control our lives. This is a concept that cognitive-behavioral therapists clearly understand—*behavioral changes begin with a change in thoughts*; therefore, Philippians 4:8 again encourages us to fix our thoughts on what is true and honorable and right, and to think about things that are pure, lovely, admirable, excellent and worthy of praise (paraphrased). Let me offer a word of encouragement: if this all seems overwhelming and you are having difficulty breaking old patterns, begin with what you **can** do. That one choice will soon fuel the desire for other positive choices. As an example, if you can't *subtract* a negative such as a bad attitude, for now, *add* Scripture study and prayer in that area. The encouragement of taking steps in a positive direction can fuel the flame to take more positive steps—positive energy creates more positive energy. A change in attitude will mean a change in action.

James 1:14-15 offers, "But each one is tempted when he is drawn away by his own desires and enticed. Then, when desire has conceived, it gives birth to sin; and sin, when it is full-grown, brings forth death." To be *drawn away* is to be enticed to do something. For instance, many know that sex outside of marriage is wrong, but the desire for sex is often stronger than the desire to obey this principle. The pull of sex is everywhere and like a fishing lure, we don't often notice the hook until we take the bait. Scan the channels on TV, view the covers of many magazines, listen to the radio, glance at the billboards that crowd our freeways and at the movie covers that fill our video stores—sex surrounds us, and it's not getting any better. Consequently, *the more we feed this desire, the more we'll have to fight this desire.* In most cases, men are vulnerable in the area of what they see and think. With that in mind, here are a few suggestions . . .

1) Avoid **looking** intentionally at things that stimulate lust. There are times when we cannot avoid what we see: a person walking by, a commercial on TV or an unannounced Internet page that suddenly emerges on the screen. Temptation is not sin, but what we do with it can be. Matthew 6:22-23 states that "The lamp of the body is the eye. If therefore your eye is good, your whole body will be full of light. But if your eye is bad, your whole body will be full of darkness. . . ." What we choose to look at determines where our thoughts will go. Determine beforehand to avoid looking at things that can stimulate lust. Not only should we pay close attention to the things we look at, but also to the things we expose our children to. For example, my wife once witnessed a man walking through the "Men's Interest Section" at a local bookstore. On the cover of a magazine were two women wearing bikinis. The man stopped, picked up the magazine and said, *"Wow, look at that,"* as he showed it to his two-year-old son. Clearly, many men are forsaking their God-intended role as spiritual leaders in the family.

2) Avoid **places** that stimulate lust. I remember reading an article about a man who learned to avoid the beach in the summer after admitting his addiction to pornography to his wife. He concluded that being around people who were barely covered often triggered his compulsion. Another case involved a man who stopped visiting certain sections at a local video store; he also concluded that viewing this material was stimulating unhealthy lust. Although these

examples may seem extreme, to reduce lust, we must avoid places, people or things that stimulate that desire. *It often begins with a small compromise, which leads to another, and another.* Simply avoid places that trigger wrong desires.

3) Avoid **saying** things that stimulate lust. Proverbs 18:21 reminds us that "Death and life are in the power of the tongue. . . ." Are your words, at times, giving life to lust? If so, rethink what you're about to say before you say it. Ask yourself if what you are about to say will strengthen your walk with the Lord, or draw you away.

4) Avoid **listening** to things that stimulate lust. Much of today's music and radio programs, for example, can be incredibly sexual in nature; they encourage thoughts that fuel unhealthy lusts. Music is a compelling force and lyrics continually place thoughts in our minds. *As thoughts grow, actions often follow.* What you choose to listen to is vitally important. Whether it's listening to others or to the media, pay close attention to whom and to what you listen to.

5) The power of **touch** creates incredible feelings. God designed this feeling to be shared within in its proper context. If married, pay close attention to friendly gestures involving other women. This may seem overstated, but again, we often make concessions in the little things. One of the best ways to control desire is by controlling touch.

If single, many view dating or courting as a license to touch without restriction. Not only is it important to place boundaries around what we see, hear and say, we also need to be careful with touch. Many Christian leaders suggest that holding hands be the only type of touching a couple displays until they move into courting. After that, only light, non-sexual touching is recommended. I know this may sound radical, but extreme or not, sex starts with a touch. One touch leads to another, and another, until we make a wrong choice. Don't place the burden of self-control on the one that you are dating— demonstrate discipline in the area of abstinence. When you display this type of discipline, you compliment her as someone of great value and respect. If you respect and honor her the way God intended, you'd either gain a godly spouse or learn from the experience. However, if you misuse His gift, a potential spouse may instead become a past regret. Focus on purity regardless of your past—it's worth it.

WHEN YOU FALL—*FALL FORWARD*

If we could clearly see where sin was leading, most of us would probably reconsider our options. The enemy blinds us to the consequences of sin and entices us with its pleasures. If one could see that one, "harmless" little sexual sin would lead to adultery, divorce, separation from children, depression and despair, he or she would probably change the behavior in a heartbeat. *We're often too smart to take large, deliberate plunges, but we can be enticed to take one step at a time, one compromise at a time, one sin at a time—until it's too late!*

When the Bible describes sin as a path that leads to death, it's describing separation from God; death simply means *separation*. Sexual sin often results in the death of a family, a marriage and the integrity of an individual. The entire family loses. That's what sin does; it draws the life out of you and those closest to you.

The enemy begins his attack with seemingly innocent activities. He'll convince us that certain movies aren't "that bad," or that adult sitcoms are "healthy entertainment." This reminds me of a story from Paul Harvey told often by Zig Ziglar. Eskimos in the barren North often kill wolves by taking a razor sharp knife and dipping it in blood. They allow the blood to freeze to the blade; then bury the handle of the knife in the snow with the blade sticking up. As the wolf begins to lick the blade, his tongue becomes desensitized due to the cold. As he continues to lick the knife, he begins to bleed, and thus, licks even faster—unaware that he is consuming his own blood and slowly killing himself. Within time, the Eskimos return to the site and bring the dead animal home. In the same way, the enemy numbs us with his deception, and our unwise choices often result in failure. Conversely, right choices promote health and success. Before making a decision, consider your choices and the outcomes, and if you fall—fall forward.

There is hope—a struggle vs. lifestyle

How can we tell if we're struggling with sin or if it has become a lifestyle? Bishop Jakes offers another excellent analogy in a series entitled *I'll Never Do That Again-The Temptation Series, 2002.* He makes the comparison of a pig and a lamb that both find their way to the mud. The mud represents the sin that all of us fall into from time to time. The pig, the person who has made sin a lifestyle, wallows in the mud and enjoys it. The lamb, the believer who struggles with sin, hates the mud and cries when he or she is stuck. That's the difference. Do you jump in and wallow around, or do you feel remorse and conviction when you step in? Again, the flesh and the spirit are constantly at war, and our choices are never free from this battle. Romans 7:25 also recognizes this struggle ". . . with the mind I myself serve the law of God, but with the flesh the law of sin." To change a lifestyle, one must apply biblical truths and avoid sinful distractions. If you're making wrong choices, STOP! Begin to make right choices and establish solid footing once again. There may be consequences, but through forgiveness there is restoration.

As a word of support, it's never too late for a new beginning. Throughout the Old Testament God continually called His people back to Him. The only command Jesus gave the woman caught in the act of adultery was that she go and sin no more (John 8:11). He didn't condemn her, criticize her or bring up the past; He gave her clear direction concerning what to do from that point forward. Yes, there are consequences for past mistakes, but it's best to live in God's arms redeemed, then to live broken outside of His will. Which way will you run?

> *It's best to live in God's arms redeemed, then to live broken outside of His will. Which way will you run?*

GUARD YOUR HEART AND IT WILL GUARD YOU

Emotions are merely a dance to the music of the heart and the dance can change with the music—not a very stable resource for making sound decisions. Our heart regulates emotions, and emotions often control actions. Proverbs 4:23 (NLT) states, "Above all else, guard your heart, for it affects everything you do."

Samson, an Old Testament character known for his strength, demonstrates the effects of giving one's heart away. The Lord blessed Samson as he grew and gave him extraordinary strength when he fought against his enemy, the Philistines. Eventually, Samson fell in love with a woman named Delilah. He confided in her and told her the source of his strength. Judges 16:16-17 (KJV) states, "And it came to pass, when she pressed him daily with her words, and urged him . . . that he told her all his heart, and said unto her, 'There hath not come a rasor upon mine head . . . if I be shaven, then my strength will go from me, and I shall become weak, and be like any other man.'"

The Philistines hated Samson and paid Delilah to trap him. When she discovered the source of his strength, she reported it to the Philistines and they took him captive. Samson failed to guard his heart, and thus, lost his strength and power, and was overthrown by the enemy.

Few things can hinder our lives more than misplaced emotions. When we are happy and positive, everything seems to go well, but when we're down and have a negative attitude, it's difficult to find the motivation to see things through. Our enemy does not want a well-guarded heart; he wants us exposed and vulnerable. He also wants us so emotionally scared from past mistakes that we spend years trying to regain lost ground.

Scripture states: *"Above all else, guard your heart. . . ."* Guarding your heart should be a priority, not a consideration. Simply stated, guard your heart and it will guard you!

To guard means to raise a protective barrier and shield our emotions. One of the best ways to guard the heart is to use both wisdom and knowledge. The Hebrew word for heart is *mind;* guarding your heart literally means guarding your mind. In short, be careful who and what you listen to, what you tell yourself and who you allow to influence you.

Knowledge is knowing what to do; wisdom is doing what you know.

> *Knowledge is knowing what to do; wisdom is doing what you know.*

For example, many know that pre-marital sex and pornography are wrong, but those who actually abstain are using both knowledge and wisdom. Many want to do what is right, but living a life of moral excellence is challenging. One can make a mental decision to abstain, but still fail, that's why guarding your heart is vastly important.

On a closing note, a few suggestions for guarding your heart are listed below. Can you add to the list?

1. Avoid compromising situations (e.g., lunch with the secretary or other female co-workers, attending company parties or functions without your wife, etc.).

2. Be alert in social situations. This includes settings such as Bible studies and prayer groups for couples, and other functions within the church.

3. Make your relationship with your wife your primary focus; second only to your relationship with God. Don't appear to enjoy the company of others—especially women—over the company of your wife.

4. Avoid discussing marital problems with the opposite sex (seek godly counsel instead).

5. Don't pursue any relationship that may compromise your integrity, or give others the wrong idea.

6. Guard your speech. Don't say things that may stimulate inappropriate desire.

7. _____

8. _____

This may sound too restrictive, but let me quote a man I respect, Zig Ziglar, who referenced another man whom I greatly respect, Billy Graham. In Zig Ziglar's autobiography, simply entitled: *Zig;* he states, "To be completely honest, I borrowed a page from Billy Graham's life and follow the same procedures he does . . . I never allow myself to be in a situation that could be misconstrued. I avoid any possibility of misunderstanding or giving the wrong impression by scrupulously watching who I am with, and how and when." A few paragraphs later, Zig adds: ". . . the Bible says that we are to avoid even the appearance of evil." I couldn't agree more. Again, *many times, the problem isn't that we raise our standard and miss it; it's that we lower it and hit it.*

Be careful. If you sense that you're in a relationship, or are building a relationship that may someday compromise your integrity, use wisdom and step away, and experience the temporary pain of discipline rather than the lasting pain of regret.

Your heart, in this sense, should be given to only one person—your wife; don't trust feelings that run opposite to this. If feelings begin to develop for a woman who is not your wife, you are heading into dangerous territory. Ask, "What does God's Word say about this situation?" not, "What do my feelings say?" Again, Proverbs 5:18 states, ". . . And rejoice in the wife of your youth." Not, "Rejoice in the wife of your youth *when you feel like it.*" Feelings can be positive if they result from choices that correspond with God's Word, but negative if they run contrary to it.

In a nutshell, at times, feelings are good and God-given, but decisions should not be made solely on feelings. Remember the study that was discussed earlier from the *Focus on the Family Newsletter* regarding couples that stayed together? The study revealed that two-thirds of the unhappily married spouses they interviewed who remained together were actually happier five years later. Undoubtedly, many of these couples didn't feel like staying together, but regardless of feelings, they remained committed to their commitment.

Wisdom for singles

References to sexual experiences in the Bible are sometimes defined as "he knew his wife." To *know,* in this context, is to know intimately through sexual experience. Regrettably, for those who experience sex before marriage, it is impossible to un-know what is known. Sexual experiences cannot be un-done. Each time we engage in premarital sex, we add additional emotional weight to our lives, and it's difficult to run a marital marathon while carrying the extra weight of regret from past relationships.

Again, weakness means the absence of strength, whereas meekness means strength under control. Those who refrain from sex before marriage exhibit far more strength than those who don't. In essence, it takes more strength to say "no" than to say "yes." Isn't that the case in so many areas of life?

As men, we are called to be the leaders in the relationship. Don't place the burden of leadership on the one you are dating— demonstrate self-control in the area of abstinence. When we display this type of discipline, we compliment her as someone of great value and respect. A word of caution to women who may be reading this, if the man you are dating is not concerned with purity (despite your past), reconsider the relationship—*if he's not concerned with doing what's right now, he may not be concerned about protecting you in other areas once married.* Although a man may find you attractive, his motivation to protect your purity, and his, should outweigh his desire for sex. If it doesn't . . . you fill in the blank.

If you've stumbled in this area, don't keep stumbling from this point forward—God will reward your obedience. There is hope and healing for those who desire it. Unmistakably, the quality of your choice today will affect the quality of your life tomorrow. If you desire a good marriage or a fulfilled single life in the future, it begins with the right choice today. For those who have chosen to postpone sexual intimacy, it will be worth the wait. Ask yourself, "Do I want to experience the temporary pain of discipline or the lasting pain of regret?"

> *The quality of your choice today will affect the quality of your life tomorrow.*

Let me restate my point. If you're currently involved in this type of relationship, understand that it's not where God wants you to be. *He cannot bless a decision to continue in a sexual relationship, which the Bible refers to as fornication, but He can bless a decision to repent and abstain until marriage.* Pre-marital sex robs the couple of a level of intimacy and closeness reserved for life-long commitment. Sex was designed by God to enhance an intimate, lasting, committed marriage.

A George Barna poll stated that 36 percent of self-proclaimed, born-again Christians approve of living together before marriage, and 39 percent said that sex before marriage is morally acceptable (*Focus on the Family* magazine, February 2002). An even larger number, despite their beliefs, have experienced sex outside of marriage. Again, why do so many Christians fall in this area? I believe that, often, *the motivation to abstain from sex does not outweigh the desire to heed God's direction.* To regain lost ground, we need to continually do those things that strengthen our relationship with Him.

The enemy desires to take what God has designed for good and distort it. It's been said *that we cannot defeat an enemy that we cannot see;* we also cannot defeat an enemy that we are not prepared for. For that reason, we're often caught off guard; therefore, it's critical to establish a commitment before a serious relationship begins, such as: "Because we have committed our relationship to God and ourselves, and because I care for you, we are not going to do . . ." Joseph ran from Potiphar's wife and cried, ". . . How then can I do this great wickedness, and sin against God?" (Genesis 39:9). He didn't say that he wasn't attracted to her; he said *how can I sin against my Lord.* His motivation to serve God was the key to his success.

His motivation to serve God was the key to his success.

One theme that appears common among the experts is this: *when we become sexually stimulated either physically or mentally, we begin to sin.* Once we are convicted within our spirit, we can rest assured that our behavior borderlines on sinful. At that point, we have the opportunity to move toward or away. Take Paul's advice and "flee sexual immorality . . ." (1 Corinthians 6:18)—flee is the key!

Again, if we respect and honor others the way God intended, we'll either gain a godly spouse or learn from the experience. However, if we misuse His gift, a potential spouse may instead become a past regret. The current trend of divorce and marital problems may be a reflection of the violation of this principle. *Becoming sexually involved before marriage does not only cloud the judgment of the couple before marriage, but can also feed thoughts of mistrust and doubt later.*

Desire will find a way, but excuses will hide it.

CHAPTER SIX

Principle

Prioritizing

Putting First Things First

When Matt was just four years old, his parents introduced him to a new friend. He was excited because he had someone to play with, and they were happy because their friend could baby-sit when they were busy.

As the years went by, Matt and his friend spent countless hours together playing video games and watching sports. In time, things changed. His friend began to use profanity and show disrespect to his family. Although his mother and father disapproved, what could they do? His friend was like a family member now. He taught Matt how to dress, how to act and even how to treat others; and although his parents wouldn't admit it, he taught them a thing or two as well. He promoted the importance of career and money; he encouraged Matt's mom to pursue her dreams outside the home, and his father to continue his pursuit of financial success. Sadly enough, they listened to his advice; as a result, Matt rarely saw his parents.

Once Matt reached his teen years, his friend's influence was obvious. Matt spent more time with him than with his family. Since Matt's dad was always gone, his friend taught him how to be a father and a husband, and since his mom was busy most of the time, he offered to teach Matt about women, and how to treat them.

When Matt was fourteen, his friend introduced him to sex. He explained how it wasn't a bad thing; everybody was doing it, even with same sex partners. At this point, Matt's parents became upset and warned Matt not to see his friend again, but he couldn't end the relationship—he'd been his close companion for the past decade. Surprisingly, Matt's parents allowed his friend to continue to live in their home. After all, they enjoyed his company and didn't really want to see him leave—he was a great entertainer.

During the years that followed, Matt's friend introduced him to alcohol, drugs and pornography, and again assured him that everyone was doing it. Matt could see his friend's point; he showed him literally thousands of people who agreed with this lifestyle.

When Matt grew older, he looked back over the years and saw that the friendship should never have continued. He believed that his friend's influence encouraged his father's affair, his mom's problem with alcohol and it may have ultimately contributed to their divorce. His friend's impact on his life was just as devastating.

Today, with full knowledge of the damage done, Matt still allows his friend to live with him, and amazingly, he still listens to his advice. Matt's friend has a name: it's *television*.

Family Friend again proves a powerful point, "For as he thinks in his heart, so is he . . ." (Proverbs 23:7). Seriously consider how you prioritize your time, and how your children will spend their time. Some believe that TV reflects society more than it influences it, and that we should strengthen the listener rather than silence the messenger, however, the following points suggest otherwise . . .

➢ On average, American families watch over seven hours of TV a day. Yes, seven hours! The book, *TV—The Great Escape*, confirms that most television programs are reshaping the moral structure of our society by lowering the standards in which we view others and ourselves.

➢ TV programs often undermine respect and the integrity of individuals.

➢ Television takes quality time from relationships, mainly marriages, and ongoing investments with children. In brief, television, on average, fills the mind with an unproductive, unrealistic outlook on life. (For those who are skeptical that the media influences our actions, consider why companies pay millions of dollars for commercials during the Super Bowl.)

Try this simple test, the next time you watch television ask . . . *does watching these commercials and/or programs strengthen my relationship with the Lord and my wife, or weaken it?* The answer will be obvious. Am I suggesting that you clear your homes of television? That's for you to decide. If you do decide to enjoy it on occasion, I suggest watching it sparingly, and view programs that offer healthy entertainment and important news updates. Unfortunately, that list is small, very small.

YOUR MOST IMPORTANT JOB—
'IT'S ALMOST TOO LATE'

The words, *'It's Almost Too Late,'* seemed to jump out as I glanced through the pages of the May/June, 2003 edition of *New Man* Magazine. Noted author and speaker, Josh McDowell, was being interviewed. After briefly discussing behavior versus beliefs in the lives of young people, he said something that impacted me greatly. He said that the reason why so many teens are losing ground in the area of spiritual truth is because their parents are not involved in teaching them in word or action. He went on to say, *"One of the most common questions I get is, 'How could we [teens] live for Christ, when we don't want the Christ that our*

> *"One of the most common questions I get is, 'How could we [teens] live for Christ, when we don't want the Christ that our parent's have?'"*

parent's have?'" Wow! What a powerful statement. A few decades ago, being a devoted parent was viewed as the most important job one could have. Society understood the famous quote *"The hand that rocks the cradle is the hand that rules the world"* (W. R. Wallace), and thus, promoted parenthood. Qualities such as honesty, integrity, commitment, discipline and a strong work ethic are not easily taught or transmitted through mere words; they are instilled through lives that model these traits. The involvement of both parents in the lives of their children helps to impart values through modeled behavior. While growing up, I took a temporary detour from God's Word. However, my parents' examples left an indelible impression. I'll be forever thankful for the time we shared, the lessons I learned and the person I became as a result of the time we spent together. *Never underestimate the power of parenting— even if you are a single parent!*

Make no mistake about it, we live in a society that emphasizes wealth and what we possess, and we often fail to remember that

> *Success is not measured by what we have, but rather by what we give.*

these things have no eternal value. I don't remember my father's income or many of the physical things my parents gave to me. I do, however, remember the values they taught—those things that money cannot buy. They taught me that success is not measured by what we have, but rather by what we give. It's been well stated: *"the best things in life aren't things."*

It's possible to succeed in business but fail at home. Look around, it's happening everywhere, from the pulpit to the boardroom. Unfortunately, the price of success is often paid at the expense of the family. A friend, Pastor Jim Girdlestone, relayed a tragic story. He told of a trip to the hospital to visit a man who was dying. The man could no longer speak, he could, however, write. His desire was to be taken off life-support, but what followed was more devastating.

The man cried as he wrote. At the top of his list, he regretted that he had not spent more time with his family. He was in anguish over the fact that he had not been a better father, but instead, had built his life around other things. When all is said and done, it is devastating to find that life was invested in those things that hold no lasting value. I encourage you, today, not to give your children a self-help book or a lecture, or to simply drop them off at church, but more importantly, *have your children desire the Christ they see in you.*

Some research indicates that the average American father actually "listens" to his children only minutes a day. A decision on our part to maintain proper priorities can solve that problem. Don't let the pursuit of career take precedence over your family. Be deliberate in planning time with your family—*if you don't schedule time, it will schedule for you.*

Our careers and hobbies, although important, should be third in priority following a relationship with God and our family. It's often said . . . if you want a true assessment of your priorities, simply check your calendar and checkbook. Do they need readjusting?

> *If you want a true assessment of your priorities, simply check your calendar and checkbook.*

THE NUMBER ONE EXCUSE

Ironically, "time" prevents us from putting first things first. How often have we said or have heard others say that they don't have enough time in their day to do this or that? I want to challenge those, who like myself, do have time to put first things first. We often forget just how precious time is. How many weeks, months or even years do we waste because we don't prioritize our lives? We need to be very careful when we say that we don't have enough time, because what we are sometimes saying is that it's not important enough.

I'm amazed at how many men "don't have time" for their family, but find time to play golf, watch television, pursue their hobbies or go out with friends. I've fallen into this trap myself and I've noticed that the real issue isn't time itself, but rather how we choose to spend it. People often ask me how I find the time to write books. I reply, "I don't attempt to *find* time, I try to prioritize my time." If the average American family has the television on seven hours a day, it's safe to assume that an individual can easily spend two hours a day or sixty hours a month watching TV. Instead of watching television, I often write, and within six months, I finish a book. Obviously, as my responsibilities increase, finding the time to write becomes more challenging, but the principle still applies— if we don't schedule time, time will schedule us. *Time is not like money; it can't be earned, borrowed or saved. You do, however, spend it, so spend wisely.*

If we don't schedule time, time will schedule us.

In essence, success is about leading a productive, balanced life, using time wisely. Desire will find a way, but excuses will hide it; therefore, it's important to get rid of excuses and prioritize your day. Ask yourself, "What's the most important thing for me to do in any given hour?" For example, contrary to what many think, reading the Bible and praying actually helps with the utilization of time. They aid in the area of discipline, patience, peace, joy and self-esteem. I've also found that my time, like money, is multiplied when I give first to God. Social life, business life and personal life all benefit from making spiritual growth a priority. *If I'm too busy to pray or read the Bible—I'm too busy!* For those who commute or drive routinely, try listening to the Bible on tape or CD. This can also be done while exercising, or with other activities; it's simply a matter of prioritizing.

Prioritizing means putting first things first. Consider finances; tithing is crucial, but sometimes difficult. Developing strong relationships with family is crucial, but sometimes difficult. Getting and staying fit is crucial, but sometimes difficult. This shouldn't surprise us, Proverbs 14:23 states, "In all labor there is profit, but idle chatter leads only to poverty." Labor is another word for "effort"; idle is another word for "inactivity." Again, effort produces results; inactivity doesn't! Putting first things first leads to success because those things in life worth having generally take energy and commitment to achieve.

All this talk about priorities, discipline, perseverance, commitment and making wise choices can be overwhelming, but you will find that they will actually increase your sense of control and overall well-being. Take small steps, and *focus on the goal of character development rather than on the process of change.*

OUR FIRST PRIORITY—IT MAY SURPRISE YOU

When I met Morgan, I recognized the need to exercise love the way God, not society, defines it. I needed to work on patience, kindness and serving, and to begin to trust, believe in her and to protect her. Love doesn't say, "That's your problem, deal with it." It says, "How can I help you in this area?" *Love is a choice, not a feeling.*

If love is the greatest commandment, it should be our first priority. When our view of love is misunderstood, we get into trouble. Ideally, attraction continues throughout marriage, however the spiritual essence of love gives it holding power.

The Bible defines love, *"Love is patient, love is kind. It does not envy, it does not boast, it is not proud. It is not rude, it is not self-seeking, it is not easily angered, it keeps no record of wrongs. Love does not delight in evil but rejoices with the truth. It always protects, always trusts, always hopes, always perseveres"* (1 Corinthians 13:4-7 NIV). This is how we are to love . . . our spouses, our friends, our children and so on.

Love is patient, love is kind.

We should be patient and understanding with the needs of others. This could simply mean being patient as your partner takes twice as long as you to get ready to go, or it may require more patience as they work through their weaknesses. Patience means taking time to be supportive and understanding, and not allowing our needs to get in the way of their needs. I know that it can be challenging at times, but it can be done. There are times, however, when you may need to talk to your partner when her requests or expectations seem unreasonable. Reserve a night to share what's on your minds, in a non-threatening manner. Both should allow the other to talk with no interruptions. Truly listen and try to understand the other's needs. There is wise counsel in the words, *seek first to understand and then to be understood.* Repeat back what is said to make sure that what is said is what is heard. We're often misunderstood and we sometimes fail to meet the need of another for a practical reason rather than a selfish motive.

Love does not envy or boast, nor is it proud.

When the spirit of envy enters our heart, it's difficult to love the way God intended. In the marriage relationship, *envy or jealousy can occur when couples view their relationship as competition rather than a commitment to cooperate.* This can happen when two people are actively involved together in ministry, school or careers. If not careful, they may compete with one another rather than pursue their dreams together. Encourage the success of one another as well as the success of the relationship.

Keep no record of wrong, nor delight in evil.

Relationships are like checking accounts. Words of healing and praise are deposits into our emotional bank account; words of anger and insults are withdrawals. If there are more withdrawals than deposits, the account not only loses value but it can create emotional bankruptcy. Emotional bankruptcy happens frequently in marriage. Learn to make deposits and avoid withdrawals if you want the highest yield from your relationship. We're human and, from time to time, we say and do things that hurt others. Others say and do things that hurt us. God instructs us to overlook the wrongs done against us, and hopefully others will do the same; keep the account open. (I'm not referring to allowing chronic physical, emotional or verbal abuse. If

> *If there are more withdrawals than deposits, the account not only loses value but it can create emotional bankruptcy.*

this is a problem, seek help from those who will give scriptural counsel, and never underestimate the power of prayer.)

Sometimes we attack one another with our words, and although done in humor, words carry enormous weight. If a wife is continually called lazy or bothersome, her self-esteem will eventually deteriorate and the relationship will lose its value. One very common, indirect insult is to ask your spouse what she has done all day. The Bible directs us to ". . . be slow to speak . . ." (James 1:19). God wants us to think before we speak and/or respond.

Love always hopes, trusts, protects and perseveres.

Hope means to anticipate, expect or to look forward to something. Love hopes for and believes the best in others. It is translated through our actions and our words. We may not always see the best in others, but we trust that it is there and we encourage it to grow.

> *We may not always see the best in others, but we trust that it is there and we encourage it to grow.*

We want to develop the type of love that protects, defends and guards the self-esteem and integrity of others.

Finally, perseverance is the principle that holds us together. It is the "stick-to-it-iveness" that binds us together during hard times. If you are single, let me take the opportunity, at this point, to address the harm in living together before marriage. The cultural concept of living together does not allow for perseverance. In essence, it states that there is no need to work through challenges because there is no solid commitment. Without a commitment to "work-through," individuals move from relationship to relationship and never allow time to develop a strong union. *Working through* challenges is the very ingredient that builds lasting relationships.

Couples today often want the freedom to divorce and leave the marriage if it doesn't work out; again, marriage never works out, you have to work it out. Living together fails to offer this most important factor, and thus, defeats itself.

> *Make love your top priority—it will not rise to that level left alone.*

True love is first a commitment to another to be patient, kind and to serve, despite emotional highs and lows. Make love your top priority—it will not rise to that level left alone.

AN OFTEN-OVERLOOKED PRIORITY

We cannot forget the importance of our health when it comes to prioritizing. It's ironic . . . we have more fitness centers, more personal trainers, more books and more articles written about fitness than ever before, yet health related illnesses and problems caused from obesity are increasing at an alarming rate. Many times, cultural programming, in the case of nutrition, runs contrary to principles that promote "good health." For instance, as I was sitting in a popular café editing this book, a group of teenagers walked in before school and ordered extra large, chocolate coffee drinks topped with caramel and whipped-cream. No wonder teens (and adults) are experiencing extremely low energy levels, attention deficit disorders and mood swings, to name only a few. Unfortunately, this was probably considered breakfast for them. It's no secret why depression, obesity and poor health are on the rise—we

> *Choosing to follow a healthier lifestyle regardless of what today's culture promotes is the first step in making health a priority.*

are not feeding our bodies what they need to function properly. Choosing to follow a healthier lifestyle regardless of what today's culture promotes is the first step in making health a priority.

Knowing the ingredients in the foods that you consume is crucial to health as well as weight-loss. *The purpose of food is to meet our nutritional needs, not our wants.* That bears repeating: food was designed to meet our needs not our wants. Many of

America's most popular foods have little, if any, nutritional value, and contain harmful ingredients. A controversial sweetener, Aspartame, for example, is used in many products (e.g., diet drinks, yogurt, gum, meal replacement shakes, supplements, etc.). Research has shown that although Aspartame is sweet, the adverse effects can be very detrimental to health. It was discovered in 1965 when Dr. Schlatter, while working on an anti-ulcer medication, mixed a substance with methanol (wood alcohol). The result was a very sweet taste. The FDA has been reviewing this additive for many years and the reports have been startling. Should we, especially our children, be consuming these types of things? You be the judge!

In Dr. Ted Broer's book, *Maximum Energy*, he lists Aspartame as one of the top ten foods and/or ingredients to avoid completely. Other ingredients include *sodium nitrites* (primarily found in luncheon meat), and hydrogenated and partially hydrogenated oils. This information should cause one to seriously reconsider the use of such products—it becomes obvious why cancer now affects one out of three individuals. Clearly, the enemy not only attacks us spiritually, but physically as well.

I encourage you to read *food labels*, and to know exactly what you're consuming. Trust me—you'll be shocked. Many of the additives found in food today are simply there to enhance flavor, coloring and appearance, and to substantially increase the shelf life of the product. Unfortunately, this approach is often far from healthy. We were created to consume living, life sustaining, God-given foods that nourish and support a healthy body. Not dead, life-depleting food from a factory.

Many of our nation's diseases are related to nutrition. It's been said that we are exposed to cancer cells daily. The best way to destroy cancer is with God-given food. I can say without a doubt that poor nutrition is one of America's deadliest habits. It's a constant challenge because it's always before us. Ask, *"Does my body need it—or does it want it?"* If it needs it, consume it. If it wants it, think twice. Often, it's not if poor nutrition causes

Often, it's not if poor nutrition causes damage, but when.

damage, but when. *What a sad commentary on the lifestyle of a nation that has such great potential to live in the blessing God has so graciously given.*

Many people spend most of their lives trying to look different, or be like someone else. They rate their appearance by society's standard. They search for fulfillment, striving to look like the perfect "ten." Unfortunately, this false perception causes many people to remain unfulfilled, even the "ten's." When we compare ourselves to one another, in doing so we are not wise. You were not designed to be someone else; you were masterfully designed to be you. If you're trying to be someone else, you may miss God's plan for *your* life.

A perfect physique does not guarantee happiness anymore than a good mattress guarantees sleep. True happiness does not come from outer appearance; it comes from spiritual health. Physical fitness, however, clearly helps.

On a final note

Little disciplines, practiced day-by-day, produce winning results. Again, we play like we practice.

First priorities should be our health and those things that build godly character (e.g., Bible reading, serving others, praying and associating with those who seek to maintain spiritual standards). The priorities you set today can be the life you enjoy tomorrow.

The priorities you set today can be the life you enjoy tomorrow.

At times, challenges are God sent; at other times, they may be the direct result of sin or a violation of spiritual principles. Determine where you turned left instead of right. From time to time you may not know why certain challenges arise, they may simply be opportunities for growth. Trust and obedience will help you stay on course during those times when nothing seems clear—simply continue to put first things first.

PRIORITIZING

In your journal, develop a list of priorities, and arrange your schedule within this framework. Briefly list your top ten priorities such as spiritual growth, family, health and career. List also what you feel they should be.

EXAMPLE:

Date: _____

What they are currently: What my top ten priorities should be:

1. _____   1. _____

2. _____   2. _____

3. _____   3. _____

4. _____   4. _____

5. _____   5. _____

6. _____   6. _____

7. _____   7. _____

8. _____   8. _____

9. _____   9. _____

10. _____   10. _____

What immediate changes can be made to correct your current order? In thirty days, list your priorities again and compare with those you established thirty days prior.

. . . and the lectures you deliver may
be very wise and true;
But I'd rather get my lesson by
observing what you do.
For I may misunderstand you and
the high advice you give,
But there's no misunderstanding
how you act and how you live.

Edgar A. Guest
"Sermons we see" from the book, The Light of Faith.

CHAPTER SEVEN

Principle

Character

Character—A Lifetime to Build, Seconds to Destroy

Building has been booming in Southern California for as long as I can remember, and contractors are often very careful in preparing the ground and laying the foundation before a building is constructed.

Although the cost to build a strong foundation is expensive, a weak foundation could cost more. Without proper support, a structure may not be sound and could present future problems. Developers hire engineers, appoint a contractor, pay fees to the city, develop a set of plans and use heavy equipment to move tons of dirt, all to prepare the foundation. In the same way, our character provides the foundation on which we build our lives.

Many spend years rebuilding simply because their foundation is weak. Companies who neglect the foundation can, in the end, spend millions of dollars reinforcing, restoring and rebuilding.

In the same way, we may spend years rebuilding and restoring our lives if we neglect our foundation.

It's unfortunate that society focuses largely on external factors such as looks, money, position or status. These superficial values have left our nation in a moral, and a spiritual crisis. It's little wonder that godly character is declining in America—our foundation as a nation, and as individuals, has slowly deteriorated.

Since recommitting my life to Christ, one of my prayers has been to continually focus on character development, but I had no idea what I was asking. Imagine a man entering the Marine Corps; he knows he wants to be a Marine but has no idea what to expect. The countless hours of training, the ongoing testing and the discipline to remain committed eventually pay off and he graduates a Marine. Was the process easy? Hardly! It was the most difficult training he'd ever faced. One doesn't merely attend boot camp for a few days, take a test and go home; the process is rigorous and intense. Likewise, when God develops character, He does so to meet the challenges ahead and to prepare us for life.

We are also tested, trained and disciplined, but the rewards far outweigh the struggles. How do we develop patience if we're not tested? How do we develop forgiveness if we are never wronged? How do we learn to trust God if we're never in need? Trying times are often intended to build us up not break us down. James 1:2-4 states, "My brethren, count it all joy when you fall into various trials, knowing that the testing of your faith produces patience. But let patience have its perfect work, that you may be perfect and complete, lacking nothing." Focus on character more than comfort and you'll be happy with the outcome.

> *Trying times are often intended to build us up not break us down.*

STUDY GUIDE

SEVEN PRINCIPLES TO LIVE BY

I remember a news story involving an enormous oil tanker that sprang a leak off the coast of Spain and millions of gallons of oil gushed out into the sea. It was a horrific site and an environmental disaster. The oil tanker was defenseless against the spill because it was full of oil. In the same way, when an individual is struck, what's inside spills out and character is revealed. When you're struck, does anger, pride or selfishness spill out, or does adversity reveal patience, forgiveness, commitment, peace, and/or perseverance? With that said, let's do a cargo check . . .

The following pages focus on character development by summarizing key points from each chapter. On the first day of each week, re-examine principle one and the key points within that section. On the second day, revisit principle two, and so on. Learning to make good choices is an important step in establishing long-term success and developing integrity. You've made a choice to change. That change will soon produce new habits that, according to research, can be developed in as little as 21 days. Stay with it, and again, *when you fall . . . fall forward!*

(I encourage you to read each chapter in the book thoroughly and resist the tendency to skip ahead to this section. All of the chapters contain useful information, much of which is not included in the following pages.)

CHAPTER ONE

Choosing to Change from the Inside Out.

Key point: We cannot successfully change our behavior without first changing the inner condition of our heart. A temporary solution cannot solve a long-term problem. Don't be fooled by thinking you can't make a difference—you can; society changes as individuals change!

1. Knowing about someone is not knowing someone. Do you have a personal relationship with Jesus Christ? If not, now is the time to make that commitment, or re-commitment.

2. Your past is forgiven, your present secure and your future certain; through Christ you are a new person. How can this thought be your buffer against ongoing discouragement?

3. Many Christian men know Scripture but they often do not apply it to their lives. How can you begin applying God's Word to your life (e.g., put the needs of your family first, spend time each morning in prayer and Bible reading, etc.)?

4. Accepting Christ isn't the finish line it's the starting point. How will you continue to run the race and finish strong?

5. Weakness is the absence of strength; meekness is strength under control. It takes far more strength to be a man of God, than to live a life void of His presence. Do you agree?

6. The foundation we build today provides the strength that weathers the storm tomorrow. In what ways can you begin to strengthen and support your foundation as a leader, a husband or as a father?

7. Are you focused on provision instead of prosperity, wisdom instead of wealth and character instead of charisma? If not, how can you realign the order?

CHAPTER TWO

Knowledge.

Key point: Biblical principles and godly wisdom are available to us, but it's our choice whether we choose to use them or not. God's Word empowers us to move forward, and helps us realize that the obstacles ahead are not greater than His power to take us through.

1. In what areas can you begin to make wisdom and knowledge a priority? Do you agree that integrity should be at the forefront of every decision?

2. Many do not make an *ongoing* spiritual investment in a lifestyle that promotes a healthy marriage. How will you be different?

3. We need to learn to pray for our wives rather than to get angry, to understand rather than become impatient and to love unconditionally rather than walk away. Any thoughts?

4. If single, how can you begin to develop positive traits now that will lead to a healthy marriage later?

5. How important is a teachable spirit? Why?

6. Do you believe that you are entrusted with gifts, whether financially, relationally or physically, and that God will reward you as you honor others?

7. Before you speak, is it important to ask, "Are my words going to build the other person up or tear them down?"

8. If a challenging decision needs to be made, let integrity guide you, not profit. Any comments?

9. Are there any relationships in your life that are pulling you down? If so, what needs to be done? Remember, desire alone doesn't guarantee success, application does.

10. Do you agree that a key component to success is knowledge, and that God's Word is the ultimate source of knowledge?

CHAPTER THREE

Choose Discipline Over Regret.

Key point: Discipline allows us to control our actions rather than allowing our actions to control us. Ask yourself this simple question before making a decision that may compromise your character, "Do I want to experience the temporary pain of discipline or the lasting pain of regret?" The answer will be clear.

1. Is discipline simply the power to put choice into action? If so, what areas can you begin putting choice into action?

2. Do you agree that you can't change where you've been, but that you can change where you're going?

3. A husband may want a large home, expensive toys and a huge bank account, but that's not what his wife needs. She needs to first feel a sense of emotional security, attention, understanding, compassion and a relationship with her husband. Do you agree that *needs* and *wants* are vastly different?

4. Do you believe that finding purpose in life is not just about reaching a destination? How can you begin, or continue to make the best of every opportunity? (Challenges can also be used as opportunities for growth.)

5. Do you agree that many people search for purpose and meaning in material possessions and other things that have no eternal value? Why is this counterproductive, and how will you be different?

6. Do you often measure happiness by your circumstances? How can this hinder peace and joy?

7. Do you often try to do your best, or be the best?

8. Problems arise when we try to be what we are not. What abilities and gifts has God given you? Are you making the best use of them?

9. When it comes to the will of God, do you recognize that it's often not as clearly defined as a road map? Do you compare your feelings with the Word of God while patiently and quietly listening, or do you often rush ahead?

10. In what areas of your life can you set your sites on the goal and not on the challenge? (For instance, if you're trying to lose weight, focus on the end result and not on the weight-loss process itself.)

CHAPTER FOUR

Preparation.

Key point: The source of our strength comes from the food we choose—what we feed grows, and what grows becomes the dominating force within our lives. Preparation is a key ingredient to success; without it, destiny is left to chance. Preparation simply means to be ready for the challenges ahead. Remember, we play like we practice.

1. Do you agree that in order to experience victory over the enemy we need more of Christ and less of the world living within us, and that it's up to us how much of each we allow in?

2. Why do we often fail to prepare for spiritual warfare?

3. If the door of temptation swings both ways, how can you choose to exit rather than enter?

4. Why do we need to be very selective in what we watch and listen to?

5. Why, at times, do we willingly walk into the enemy's camp?

6. Do you agree that the lust of the flesh, the lust of the eyes and the pride of life are the top three things to avoid while gaining victory over temptation?

7. Are you sabotaging your success through anger, addiction or arrogance? What situations should be avoided? What changes need to be made?

8. The enemy would like us to believe that prayer is ineffective and that serving Christ is not rewarding. What can we do to offset his influence?

9. Do you agree that preparation involves being obedient in doing what is right even though there appears to be no outward evidence of results?

10. How often should we listen to Paul's advice in Philippians 4:8 (NLT), ". . . Fix your thoughts on what is true and honorable and right. Think about things that are pure and lovely and admirable. Think about things that are excellent and worthy of praise." How would you go about doing this?

CHAPTER FIVE

Wisdom: Choosing Wisely.

Key point: Although there are negative consequences for poor choices, there are also positive consequences for wise choices. If you desire a good marriage or a fulfilled life in the future, it begins with the right choice today. We're often too smart to take large, deliberate plunges, but we can be enticed to take one step at a time, one compromise at a time, until it's too late.

1. Are there areas in your life that are taking you down? If so, how can you break free?

2. We are called to be leaders in marriage and in dating relationships. In what ways can you begin or continue to fulfill this role?

3. In general, are you positioned to be drawn away by the strong pull of sin, or are you firmly footed on solid ground? In what areas do you need solid footing?

4. How can you avoid looking intentionally at things that stimulate lust? Are there places that should be avoided?

5. Is your motivation to serve God outweighing your desire to compromise? If not, what changes can be made?

6. How can you begin to, or continue to guard your heart? Revisit the suggestions on page 90. Do you notice any areas that require attention?

7. Why do *feelings* often run contrary to God's Word? Why shouldn't we trust our feelings?

8. Do you agree that the quality of choice today affects the quality of life tomorrow?

CHAPTER SIX

Prioritizing: First Things First.

Key point: Our focus should be on gaining a right perspective of God, family and career, and in that order. It's good to pursue the desires of our heart, as long as our desires are God-given and focused on helping others.

1. Do you feel that the story, *Family Friend,* presents a powerful point about outside influence? Do you agree that, "For as he thinks in his heart, so is he . . ." (Proverbs 23:7)?

2. How do our thoughts become the framework for our actions?

3. We need to be very careful when we say that we don't have enough time, because what we are sometimes saying is that it's not important. Do you agree?

4. Is this a true statement: *desire will find a way, but excuses will hide it.* How might this statement apply to spiritual disciplines?

5. Do you agree that love is a choice, not a feeling, and that we'll never find the perfect person, but with God's help, we'll find the perfect person for us?

6. Undoubtedly, if love is the greatest commandment it should be our first priority, correct?

7. Do you agree that relationships are like checking accounts, and that words of healing and praise are deposits and words of anger and insults are withdrawals? Do you have a tendency to make more deposits, or withdrawals?

8. Is health an often over-looked priority in your life? If so, what can be done to change this?

9. Comment: often, it's not "if" poor nutrition causes damage, but "when"!

Character

The previous six principles lead to the development of character. Continue reviewing chapters one through six and don't get discouraged; character is built from the struggles we face and the difficulties we overcome. Good character reflects integrity, restores relationships and influences others to look to God for support and encouragement. Our words, our actions and our habits all reflect our character. Continually look to God's Word for examples of character and integrity.

Much like dividing lines on a highway, His laws are there to protect us, not to prevent us from enjoying the journey.

Much like dividing lines on a highway, His laws are there to protect us, not to prevent us from enjoying the journey. Again, godly character can rebuild a marriage, restore a relationship and influence others to follow its lead. In contrast, bad character can ruin a marriage, destroy a relationship and draw the wrong crowd. Strive to build character rich in patience, trust, love, perseverance, commitment and godly wisdom.

The next time you're "struck," consider a cargo check and determine what areas need improvement, and make a commitment to work on them.

FINAL THOUGHTS

Succeeding the way God designed it, whether married or single, is not difficult. Establish a goal and stay committed to Him. Control your thoughts, move forward and ignore setbacks. Prioritize your time, and stay motivated. Sound difficult? Not really. Most of us already do these things. We have goals, but perhaps they're wrong or unrealistic; we're committed, but sometimes to the wrong things; we have time, but it's frequently misappropriated; we have priorities, but they're sometimes misplaced; we feed our thoughts, but often with the wrong information; and we're disciplined, but only in certain areas of our lives . . . it's all about choosing wisely!

My message is simple and straightforward: life is often a reflection of the choices we make. Only a solid biblical foundation, along with a personal relationship with Jesus Christ, can help us regain lost ground.

By now you've noticed that I've stressed the importance of daily prayer and Bible reading. Please don't make the mistake that I, and millions of others have made. Although many profess to be Christians, they are not truly committing their lives to Christ. It's been said that *if He's not Lord of all, He's not Lord at all.* No matter how hard we try, we cannot live as true followers of Christ unless the Bible and biblical principles become our primary focus. God's Word is the most important thing that we posses; it should never be taken for granted. President Jackson said of the Bible as he lay on his deathbed, "That Book, Sir, is the rock on which our Republic rests." As it is with us, God's Word is the solid rock on which our lives rest.

Although biblical principles sound difficult, they simply help us *stick to doing what is right.* Wrong choices complicate your life and rob you of peace. With that in mind, is there really any choice?

SEEK TO BE A MAN WHO . . .

As I was concluding this book, my mother handed me an old piece of paper that she wrote nearly twenty-five years ago. On it, she listed several character traits that men should strive to possess—I couldn't have chosen a better way to end this chapter on character. If you take anything from this book, I hope that it is this.

Seek to be a man who . . .

. . . above all, sincerely desires to love and serve the Lord.

. . . hungers for a righteous spirit, and is honest at all times despite the cost.

. . . chooses words and actions that are wise and well thought through; considering first the consequences, and who does not act impulsively in anger with words or actions.

. . . desires to protect, preserve, appreciate and encourage the beauty in a women, and who recognizes his strength and masculinity as created by God for a specific purpose.

. . . focuses on the needs of others rather than his own, and is not critical and domineering when communicating.

. . . works hard, and stops at nothing to accomplish what God has set before him.

. . . stretches the limits of his body, soul and spirit to excel in every area possible and to recognize those areas.

. . . desires to encourage and nurture others rather than to overpower and control.

. . . seeks excellence in all things and lives to that end.

You can't change where you've been,
but you can change where
you're going.

CHAPTER EIGHT

Divorce—Hope for the Hurting

Broken—Yet Unbreakable

As a child, I was captured by the stories that my grandfather told about life on the farm in Oklahoma in the mid 1900's. The images I've held are not those of pleasant surroundings and ideal conditions; they're impressions of twelve-hour days spent working the land, wind storms that could devastate a crop, blistered and sunburned skin and poverty unlike most Americans know today. Life, in general, was harder then, but interestingly enough, marriages seemed much stronger. It was a time when commitment, integrity and honesty stood in place of contracts, disclosures and bylaws. I'm not suggesting that we return to that time in history, but that we learn from the past and strongly encourage those same principles today.

In the past, a life-long commitment and exclusive intimacy in marriage held the family together. It was in that setting that children learned and character developed. Divorce was rarely an option, and a husband or a wife was considered an asset rather than a liability. Today's culture tends to ask, "What can I get from this relationship?" rather than, "What can I give to this relationship?"

What do you bring into a relationship? Are you willing to develop qualities that support commitment? Many focus on

Many focus on finding the "right" person without first focusing on becoming the "right" person.

finding the "right" person without first focusing on *becoming* the "right" person. The principle of *reaping* and *sowing* not only relates to financial success, but it relates to success with others as well. If one desires to find a trustworthy, honest, committed person, he or she should first offer the same. Unfortunately, marriages, families and other relationships often fail because they embrace values that promote meeting self-centered needs rather than meeting the needs of others.

With millions of Americans now classified as divorced and "newly" single, and the countless others who are contemplating divorce, the need to address this topic is unavoidable and

Life can make us bitter or it can make us better.

necessary. It's been well stated that life can make us bitter or it can make us better. Those who do not allow hurt to entrap them can turn brokenness into an unbreakable force, but those shackled by past pain are truly imprisoned by it— *the walls we build to protect us may eventually imprison us.*

How can we undo the emotional pain we experience from failed relationships? First, understand that it's not an external fight—it's an internal struggle. Our minds are battlefields where personal conflicts are either won or lost. God works within our spirits by transmitting His Word into healthy thoughts. I don't mean to discount the deep emotional and psychological pain of failed relationships, but I do want to remind you that God makes provision for all of our needs.

Second, of all the books I've read, the sermons I've heard, the couples I've talked with and the devastation I've seen firsthand, one common denominator was present: *those who do not forgive or release bitterness, anger and hurt, never experience freedom, happiness or true restoration.* Ephesians 4:31-32 states . . . "Let all bitterness, wrath, anger, clamor, and evil speaking be put away from you, with all malice. And be kind to one another, tenderhearted, forgiving one another, even as God in Christ forgave you." Simply stated, if you fail to forgive, bitterness and anger, though skillfully masked, can and will tarnish future relationships. Divorced, separated or single, God can turn brokenness into an unbreakable force, but it is imperative that your mind is renewed by applying biblical principles, beginning with forgiveness.

The word brokenness describes a variety of experiences. For the purpose of this section, we'll discuss brokenness of spirit. Brokenness resulting from the loss of a home, employment, money or other material possessions is much different from *relational* brokenness.

Years ago, I was listening to a syndicated Christian radio program during my morning run. A survivor of the holocaust was being interviewed. She described the horrific conditions of the concentration camps and then made a statement I'd never forget: *she described the emotional pain and the brokenness she experienced from her divorce as greater than the pain of the concentration camp.* Six months later, another guest on the same program, described the pain of losing her husband to cancer. She spoke about how his illness devastated their lives after ten long months of suffering. I was again moved to hear her say that she would have rather lost her husband to death by cancer than divorce. Unbelievable! Two different women who had gone through more pain than many of us will ever know said that divorce is, or would be, more painful than death. My mind searched for understanding . . . why was divorce more devastating than a concentration camp, or cancer? For several weeks I pondered this question. My answer came: death is a natural process and God makes provision, but the spiritual union of two people was never designed to be broken—the spirit is vulnerable in divorce and the pain continues. We may try to hide the pain that lingers from a broken spirit, but it's always there waiting for the opportunity to consume us. Unless God rebuilds the foundation, those divorced often find themselves in the same situation with the second, third or fourth spouse.

The good news, however, is that both of the women spoke of God's healing power. Regardless of what they had endured, God delivered them from emotional scars and feelings of abandonment. He can deliver those broken by a failed marriage as well, but *change must first occur on the inside.* Strongholds such as bitterness, pride, lust, past sexual experiences, selfishness, substance abuse, anger and physical abuse, to name a few, are among those that hinder the healing and rebuilding process. Healing begins with a commitment to work on those areas known to be detrimental to your spiritual health and relationships.

A commitment is just that—a commitment. Our attitude should be one in which we surrender our entire lifestyle to God. I've spoken with many who admitted that alcohol or substance abuse ruined their relationship, but instead of surrendering the problem to God and breaking their addiction, they simply found someone else to tolerate their habit. Unfortunately, the problem soon surfaced again. It's little wonder that many go through life changing partners, careers or residency, searching for someone or something that can never be found apart from spiritual wholeness. If this is you, I encourage you to stop wandering from relationship to relationship and allow a personal relationship with Jesus Christ to rebuild and restore you.

If you're like me, you may realize that years of "wandering" could have been avoided. Many, no doubt, had direction for their marriage, but because of selfishness, disobedience, disregard or a deaf ear to God's direction, it ended with divorce . . . but *God can rebuild and redeem that life*; He desires to guide and direct us.

God often uses brokenness to rebuild. An analogy that comes to mind is that of a shepherd. Perhaps you've heard that from time to time a shepherd might break the leg of a lamb that continually wandered from the flock, and thus, from the shepherd's protection. The shepherd would then splint the broken leg and carry the lamb on his shoulders for weeks until the leg had healed.

As painful as this was for the lamb, it was necessary to protect it from being ravished by wolves or other predators. In time, through the broken and dependant relationship, the lamb learned to walk and to remain in the protective presence of his shepherd. This was well stated by David in Psalm 51:8, ". . . That the bones You have broken may rejoice," and in Isaiah 53:6 "All we like sheep have gone astray . . ."

What will it take to bring us back to the Shepherd? A deliberate decision to stay close to the Shepherd can avoid needless pain and provide safety and protection; this is the first step in changing brokenness into an unbreakable force.

DIVORCE: WHEN TO HOLD ON, WHEN TO MOVE ON

This section was written during the single years that followed my divorce. It brought to mind the millions of people living with the consequences of a failed marriage; many may have desired to remain faithful to their commitment while their spouse chose to leave.

Life after divorce can be just "existence"—peace and joy have all but left. If this describes you, as it did me, let me assure you that God desires that peace and joy be restored. When my wife filed for divorce in 1998, as a single, I felt like half of a person that needed someone to complete me. In reality, a spouse will not complete me (or you); only God can bring wholeness and fullness to our lives. We were created as individuals, and God uses our individual qualities to glorify Him, married or single.

I often thank the Lord for using my divorce to change my direction. God was not responsible for my divorce, but He did use it to redirect me. My divorce was the result of misguided focus, primarily on my part—pride, anger and alcohol abuse eventually came to collect. That's why it's vitally important that two people enter the marriage covenant putting Christ first. Do not lose your identity in the other person, but rather develop the gifts within your God-given individuality and learn to work together.

In my case, God used my situation to change me and bring new meaning to my life. Some of the consequences of my divorce may linger, but so will His unfailing grace, mercy and love, and for that I am continually grateful.

At this point I feel the need to clarify: <u>Clearly understand that I'm not advocating divorce, nor am I suggesting that if you are currently separated, divorce become an option because better opportunities await you. As men, I believe that it is our responsibility to do everything that we can to restore our marriage and contend for the relationship.</u> God hates divorce and anyone who has been there knows why. Again, I believe, first and foremost, in reconciliation and restoration but these are not always options if things such as extreme abuse and adultery have occurred, or continue to occur. At this point, some may disagree and believe that Christians are responsible to do whatever they can to reconcile, and I agree. That's why a personal relationship with Jesus and access to His wisdom and daily guidance is profoundly important. Through that relationship you will be able to make the right decision. It won't be easy because lives have been damaged, dreams destroyed and promises broken, but God continually redeems us through His forgiveness. God desires that we get back on track and follow His lead in spite of detours. If separated, or (in some cases) divorced, don't leave the success of your marriage or reconciliation to chance. Do whatever you can to rebuild and restore your commitment to your wife.

One of the biggest obstacles when considering restoration or seeking direction is becoming involved with someone soon after you divorce or separate. This can severely hinder your chance for reconciliation, as well as your ability to follow God's lead. You might feel that this new person makes you feel loved and appreciated, and that may be true, but so did your spouse when you first met. Again, *love does not leave people—people leave love,* and until you've made changes that will

Until you've made changes that will change your future, you're bound to repeat your past.

change your future, you're bound to repeat your past.

Every situation is different and some divorces are inevitable, but for the large percentage of those who can rebuild and restore their relationship, two choices are available, to face the pain of discipline, or the pain of regret. Disciplining yourself to do the right thing is difficult, but living with the pain of regret is much harder.

As stated earlier, although I accepted Christ at an early age, the pull of the world was enticing, and I pursued many of the wrong things. Again, there is nothing wrong with having dreams, but there is a difference between having dreams and dreams having you.

As a result of my passion for worldly things, I entered into marriage with those things as first priorities and my marriage second, or third, or fourth. After four years of marriage, I succeeded financially but failed relationally. Immediately, we both sought new relationships. Our focus shifted from a failed marriage to new relationships; restoration became increasingly more difficult. If you are recently divorced, I encourage you not to move ahead in a new relationship until you have exhausted all avenues of restoration and a significant amount of time has passed. If you are separated, don't rush a divorce; and definitely do not begin a new relationship. Understand that you are about to make a big decision—a decision that will last a lifetime. Countless couples live with ongoing regret and remorse, simply because they trusted divorce for the answer rather than God and restoration. If you have been divorced for sometime and reconciliation is not an option, there still needs to be time for healing, and a new relationship, more often than not, will only mask the pain, hinder the healing process and prevent problems from being addressed.

> *Countless couples live with ongoing regret and remorse, simply because they trusted divorce for the answer rather than God and restoration.*

After spending a year searching for fulfillment through other relationships, I admitted to God that I was trying to find someone who would make me happy rather than focusing on what He wanted to do in me, and I recommitted my life to Christ. I had no idea that it would take two additional years before He brought Morgan into my life. God was not only preparing someone for me, but me for them.

Perhaps my three-year journey could have been much longer had I not committed to change. Don't be like the Israelites and allow a short journey (a matter of days) through the wilderness to become forty-years of wandering; identify your weaknesses and commit to work on them. Strengths are seen in what we stand for; weaknesses in what we fall for. Identify your weaknesses, those areas that seem to trip you time-and-time again, and sincerely seek to make changes.

> *Strengths are seen in what we stand for; weaknesses in what we fall for.*

Is restoration always God's will?

God hates divorce and reconciliation is pleasing to Him. There are instances when one is released through adultery and is no longer bound, however Jesus said in Matthew 19:8, ". . . Moses permitted divorce as a concession to your hard-hearted wickedness, but it was not what God had originally intended" (NLT). From the beginning marriage was designed to be a life-long commitment. He also states in Luke 16:18, "Anyone who divorces his wife and marries another woman commits adultery, and the man who marries a divorced woman commits adultery" (NIV). For this reason, reconciliation should be a top priority.

First and foremost, God desires that we walk in integrity, follow His principles and use wisdom during the journey. For some, reconciliation may result, for others it may not. Regardless, God still loves you, and desires to help you regain lost ground.

The enemy often resurrects past failures to prevent future success. He knows that God has plans for our lives and he seeks to undermine those plans. For instance, as Morgan and I began our relationship, when I heard sermons about letting go of the past I would become excited about our new relationship, but when I heard discussions about divorce and restoration, I became fearful—my past, was clearly preventing a hopeful future. But as we moved forward in the relationship, anxiety and confusion gave way to peace, joy and fulfillment.

> *The enemy often resurrects past failures to prevent future success.*

As a final confirmation, before I committed fully to Morgan, I contacted my former wife (nearly three years after our divorce) to validate my feelings of being released from our past relationship. She confirmed that she was in a long-term relationship that would eventually lead to marriage, and she wished me the best. I felt that I had received my last and most solid confirmation. It was now clear that I could no longer allow past brokenness to cause future pain.

Morgan and I never fully understood why we felt anxiety; it did, however, cause us to focus more intently on God and not ourselves, and when we finally committed to our marriage vow, we knew it was a binding statement representing a life-long commitment—a commitment that we both had always wanted.

If you sense that restoration is possible, and even if you don't, I encourage you to remove everything that may hinder this process such as wrong relationships, strongholds and addictions. In addition, I highly recommend the two tape audio series from pastors Jack Hayford, Scott Bauer and John Tolle entitled: *The DEVASTATING Dimensions of Divorce*. The series is artfully presented and ministers to the needs of those recovering from divorce, those currently separated and those contemplating divorce. A question and answer segment is also included. (Their website address is www.livingway.com)

When to hold on—when to move on

Again, this section was written primarily to those whose spouse has chosen to leave and they are wondering if they should hold on, or move on. Ultimately, only you, with God's help, can answer this question. It is my desire, however, that the following information will help you make the right decision.

Before making a decision of this magnitude, I offer three directives. First, discontinue any relationship that is not Christ-

centered or that may cloud your judgment. I often wonder how
many marriages are not restored simply because people immediately
become involved in other relationships and don't wait on the Lord.
Second, pray, seek godly counsel and allow God's Word to direct
you. Third, don't be in a hurry. Restoration is a process. Don't abort
the process because you're in a hurry. Healing and direction take
time and patience. If it took years to damage the marriage, it may
take years to rebuild, or for emotional wholeness to be restored.

FIVE POINTS TO CONSIDER . . .

1. Perhaps the most difficult Scripture dealing with divorce or separation
   is found in 1 Corinthians 7:10-11 "**. . . A wife must not leave her
   husband. But if she does leave him, let her remain single or else
   go back to him. And the husband must not leave the wife**" (NLT).
   This clearly states that those who are divorced and/or separated,
   unless "scripturally released," should not remarry. I believe that if this
   Scripture were fully acknowledged, it would be a deterrent to divorce
   and create more serious consideration before marriage and remarriage
   to another. There would be fewer divorces without cause and more
   reconciliation's. Lack of regard for this Scripture has taken us to the
   other extreme—no fault divorce. However, if the spouse who left is
   an unbeliever and shows no desire for reconciliation after a significant
   amount of time, verse fifteen may offer direction.

2. 1 Corinthians 7:15 states, **"But if the husband or wife who isn't a
   Christian insists on leaving, let them go. In such cases the
   Christian husband or wife is not required to stay with them, for
   God wants his children to live in peace"** (NLT). Even if this is the
   case, it's wise to allow a significant amount of time to pass before
   moving forward. This may reveal if the person left only for a
   season, or has chosen to leave permanently. Other translations of
   this verse state that a Christian is not under *bondage* in such a case.
   If someone leaves and has no intention of returning, God does not
   want us to be bound to that past relationship—He wants us to live in
   peace. In this case, I believe that marriage to another is an option,
   but as always, seek counsel and direction; always recognize God's
   Word as the ultimate source.

3. Matthew 19:9 states **"And I tell you this, a man who divorces his wife and marries another commits adultery—unless his wife has been unfaithful"** (NLT). Again, God reveals his nature concerning commitment to a spouse. Clearly, a spouse who has been unfaithful releases the other and they are no longer bound. It is unfortunate that all divorced individuals are referred to as "divorced." It might be helpful and less confusing for those whose spouse was unfaithful to be referred to as "released." Certainly unfaithfulness does not mean that the marriage cannot be restored if both the husband and wife seek God's guidance.

4. A personal favorite, 1 Corinthians 7:17 states, **"You must accept whatever situation the Lord has put you in, and continue on as you were when God first called you . . ."** (NLT). We are to use every situation for God's glory. If single, use that opportunity to build and strengthen character, and care for the things of God. If separated, use that time to seek God more fervently and pray for guidance and direction. Allow Him to mold and direct you, and rebuild the relationship. If divorced, use that experience to learn while asking what good can come from it; you may minister to others who have gone through a divorce. One of God's wonderful attributes is that He desires to use our brokenness. In fact, it is in our weakness that His strength is manifested. Be assured that all things can work together for good as we commit our lives to Him!

5. **You can't control choices others make.** You may be able to influence them or encourage them, but ultimately the choice to leave or to stay is up to them. God has given us the freedom to choose; in marriage, the choices of one can greatly affect the life of the other. If you and your spouse are apart, and you've waited and done all that you can do biblically, I believe that God looks at your heart more than your circumstance. King David was not able to build the temple because of his past—he was a man of war, but God said, ". . . Whereas it was in your heart to build a temple for My name, you did well in that it was in your heart" (II Chronicles 6:8); because David's heart was right, God counted it as righteousness. Although he did not build the temple, God looked upon him as if he had. In the same way, your marriage may not be restored, but as long as your heart is right, God will honor and bless your circumstances because you trusted in

> *In marriage, the choices of one can greatly affect the life of the other.*

Him and were obedient. He can rebuild your life and open doors you might not have thought possible. Once I recommitted my life to Christ, it changed dramatically. I went from weekend alcohol consumption and a career that wasn't God-centered, to a life nearly void of alcohol cravings, a ministry I never dreamed possible and a godly wife who has been a tremendous blessing. Did I make bad decisions along the way? Yes, I did, but I was quick to repent and seek God's help. Had I become angry and unwilling to change, only the Lord knows where I'd be today. Choose wisely today because, again, *the consequences of bad choices take us farther than we want to go, keep us longer than we want to stay and cost us more than we want to pay.*

In closing this section on divorce, I asked pastor, Sean Appleton, if he could briefly speak to those, who by no choice of their own, have experienced divorce and are feeling condemned. He stated:

"There are many views on the term 'biblical.' Sometimes a 'no tolerance' approach to ethical situations is based on a person's life experience, their understanding of God (love, forgiveness, acceptance), or a doctrinal stance they might have been exposed to. It's interesting how life has a way of tempering our theology. We certainly want to uphold the truth of God's Word, and not compromise our standards, yet our theology, at times, reflects our own attitudes toward God and toward what is right and wrong based on our personal pain. Remember what Jesus said to the Pharisees about the woman caught in adultery? Their judgments were based on their 'own' understanding of righteousness, not on God's. And remember the woman who wiped Jesus' feet with her hair and tears? Jesus responded to their judgments on her past sins by commenting on her understanding of God's love. (He who is forgiven much, loves much.) Many dissect the letter of the law and miss the heart of God."

SEVEN WAYS TO REBUILD AFTER BROKENNESS

As I was completing *What Works for Singles,* I was asked to speak to a group of singles in Southern California. Ironically, the topic was *Rebuilding After Brokenness.* In prayerful preparation for this message, I isolated seven ways to rebuild based on the story of Nehemiah found in the Old Testament.

I. **Fast and pray:** Nehemiah 1:4 states, "So it was, when I heard these words, that I sat down and wept, and mourned for many days; I was fasting and praying before the God of heaven." Nehemiah discovered that the Jews who survived the captivity were living in great distress and that the wall of Jerusalem that had represented their strength had been destroyed. Nehemiah understood that the first step was prayer and fasting. *Fasting forces us to neglect the flesh and feed the spirit;* it's a time to focus on God's Word. Fasting and prayer together release spiritual strength not otherwise available.

II. **Confess:** In verses six and seven Nehemiah prays, ". . . we have sinned against You. Both my father's house and I have sinned. We have acted very corruptly against You, and have not kept the commandments . . ." Although our brokenness may have resulted from the actions of another, we are never above reproach. Confession, prayer and fasting, are often the beginning steps that open the door for God's redeeming power.

Confession, prayer and fasting, are often the beginning steps that open the door for God's redeeming power.

III. **Return to God:** This should be the first thing we do. In verses eight and nine, Nehemiah quotes God's commandment to Moses, ". . . If you are unfaithful, I will scatter you among the nations; but if you return to Me, and keep My commandments and do them, though some of you were cast out to the farthest part of

God reminds us that if we return to Him, and keep His commandments, He will bring us to a place of restoration (even in our marriages).

the heavens, yet I will gather them from there, and bring them to the place which I have chosen as a dwelling for My name. . . ." One of the leading causes of divorce in America is sexual unfaithfulness, but there is a solution. God reminds us that if we return to Him, and keep His commandments, He will bring us to a place of restoration (even in our marriages). Whether we were the cause of the brokenness or were primarily on the receiving end, we must return to God and His commandments.

IV. **Position yourself to rebuild:** Nehemiah said to the king ". . . If it pleases the king, and if your servant has found favor in your sight, I ask that you send me to Judah, to the city of my fathers' tombs, that I may rebuild it" (2:5). Nehemiah didn't leave for Judah without first positioning himself by asking the king to bestow favor. He knew that he would need resources, men and the king's blessing to accomplish the task of rebuilding the wall. To position ourselves means *to align or arrange our lives in such a way that we are able to receive God's blessings.* During this step, remove everything that does not correspond with God's Word. For example, if you're praying for restoration in your marriage, or seeking a godly spouse, don't live promiscuously. If you're in the healing stages, resurrecting past memories and regrets is not wise—positioning yourself in the center of God's will is your primary focus.

V. **Use new things to build:** In Nehemiah 2:8, we read that Nehemiah requested new lumber for the rebuilding of the wall, the gates and his home. Although he used old stones from the previous wall, Nehemiah also needed new material to rebuild the new wall. In the same way, God will bring new things into your life; be open to change. *How do you know when your past is affecting your future?* If your plans, hopes and dreams are drawing from the past and preventing change, your past may be affecting your future. For instance, for several months after I met Morgan, I was not able to move forward in our relationship. My divorce, although years earlier, was still haunting me. Morgan was the first woman I courted since my divorce, and trust and marital failure were issues I had to resolve before we moved forward—I needed to be open for change.

VI. Hold it in your heart: This step refers mainly to those who are in the critical restoration and rebuilding stages of a marriage. Nehemiah 2:12 states, "Then I arose in the night, I and a few men with me; I told no one what my God had put in my heart to do at Jerusalem. . . ." When God places something in your spirit, *it's best not to disclose immediately,* simply ponder it in your heart. If you're sensing restoration in your spirit, at times, it's best not to share this with your ex-spouse just yet. A true story involved a wife who left her husband. During the separation, he called her nearly every day, sent dozens of flowers and wrote letters every week telling her how God was going to restore their marriage. After nearly a year, his wife filed for divorce and moved away. When asked if she considered reconciliation, she stated that she considered it many times but because of his constant pressure for restoration, she felt stifled and inclined to move farther away. Dr. Dobson's book, *Love Must Be Tough,* refers to this as *opening the cage door.* When a spouse who feels smothered or fenced in wants to leave (or has left), it's wise to open the cage door and release him or her. Although not true of every situation, time away allows them to reconsider their marriage, and reconciliation may then become an option. The husband previously mentioned actually contributed to his wife's decision to leave by never opening the cage door. *Don't be a "velcro man" in a relationship, a marriage or attempting to restore one—use wisdom and patience.*

VII. Expect opposition: As you begin to rebuild and restore your life, expect opposition. Nehemiah 2:19 says, ". . . they laughed at us and despised us. . . ." The enemy will oppose us any way that he can. He'll use pessimistic people and/or fill our minds with negative thoughts in an attempt to distract us from reaching our goal. Again, don't allow people's opinions to become your reality unless they are positive. Those trying to rebuild a marriage may be taunted by the thought, "It's useless—why try?" Those trying to rebuild a broken past may often think, "I've done too much damage—why try, God can't use me now." The enemy emphasizes the negative and attempts to conceal the positive. Nehemiah responded in verse twenty, ". . . the God of heaven

Himself will prosper us; therefore we His servants will arise and build. . . ." Nehemiah understood that *God Himself would oversee the building project regardless of the damage or the hostility.* Once Nehemiah overcame his critics, his opposition became even greater. Nehemiah 4:3 states ". . . Whatever they build, if even a fox goes up on it, he will break down their stone wall," and verse eight adds, "and all of them conspired together to come and attack Jerusalem and create confusion." Nehemiah's opposition increased as he continued to obey God, but he understood that if God was for him no one could stand against him, and he eventually rebuilt the wall. Likewise, God is greater than the problem you're facing. The key is to focus on what He can and will do in your life even though no evidence is seen. Hebrews 11:1 reminds us that ". . . faith is the substance of things hoped for, the evidence of things not seen." Faith believes God's promises before they happen. Simply stated, **stay focused on the goal not the opposition.**

As you rebuild, I encourage you to wait on the Lord, obey His Word, seek guidance through counsel and allow God to work in your life. Ask, trust and move forward. God's lead is usually not as direct as we'd like; however, it is certain. Again, ask for wisdom and guidance and make sure that your decision agrees with Scripture, then take that step of faith. *The steps of faith fall on the seemingly void, but find the rock beneath* (Whittier). You may feel that you're walking blindly in to the void, but as you step out and trust, you'll find the rock beneath.

"The choice is up to us. Do we passively stand-by while marriages are being shattered and families destroyed, or do we engage the enemy and rebuild our nation on solid biblical ground? It's not too late. But before we can rebuild our nation, we must first restore the family; and before we restore the family, we must first strengthen the individual—it all begins with each of us."

—Shane Idleman, 2002

Other resources from *El Paseo Publications,*
including
What Works When "Diets" Don't
and
What Works for Singles,
are available through
www.elpaseopublications.com
and
www.whydietsdontwork.com

Future releases include:
**What Works for Teens—Solid Choices
In Unstable Times**
and
**What Works When Leadership Fails—From
Desecration to Consecration.**

JOURNAL NOTES

*Date*_____

Today's thoughts . . . _____

_____

_____

_____

_____

I was reminded of the Scripture that says . . . _____

_____

_____

_____

_____

How can I begin or continue to apply this verse to my life? . . .

_____

_____

_____

_____

Prayer requests . . . _____

_____

_____

_____

Answers to prayers . . . _____

_____

_____

_____

JOURNAL NOTES

*Date*_____

Today's thoughts . . . _____

_____

_____

_____

_____

I was reminded of the Scripture that says . . . _____

_____

_____

_____

_____

How can I begin or continue to apply this verse to my life? . . .

_____

_____

_____

_____

Prayer requests . . . _____

_____

_____

_____

Answers to prayers . . . _____

_____

_____

_____

JOURNAL NOTES

*Date*_____

Today's thoughts . . . _____

_____

_____

_____

_____

I was reminded of the Scripture that says . . . _____

_____

_____

_____

_____

How can I begin or continue to apply this verse to my life? . . .

_____

_____

_____

_____

Prayer requests . . . _____

_____

_____

_____

Answers to prayers . . . _____

_____

_____

_____

JOURNAL NOTES

*Date*_____

Today's thoughts . . . _____

_____

_____

_____

_____

I was reminded of the Scripture that says . . . _____

_____

_____

_____

_____

How can I begin or continue to apply this verse to my life? . . .

_____

_____

_____

_____

Prayer requests . . . _____

_____

_____

_____

Answers to prayers . . . _____

_____

_____

_____

JOURNAL NOTES

*Date*_____

Today's thoughts . . . _____

_____

_____

_____

_____

I was reminded of the Scripture that says . . . _____

_____

_____

_____

_____

How can I begin or continue to apply this verse to my life? . . .

_____

_____

_____

_____

Prayer requests . . . _____

_____

_____

_____

Answers to prayers . . . _____

_____

_____

_____

JOURNAL NOTES

*Date*_____

Today's thoughts . . . _____

_____

_____

_____

_____

I was reminded of the Scripture that says . . . _____

_____

_____

_____

How can I begin or continue to apply this verse to my life? . . .

_____

_____

_____

_____

Prayer requests . . . _____

_____

_____

_____

Answers to prayers . . . _____

_____

_____

_____

JOURNAL NOTES

*Date*_____

Today's thoughts . . . _____

_____

_____

_____

_____

I was reminded of the Scripture that says . . . _____

_____

_____   _____

_____

How can I begin or continue to apply this verse to my life? . . .

_____

_____

_____

_____

Prayer requests . . . _____

_____

_____

_____

Answers to prayers . . . _____

_____

_____

JOURNAL NOTES

Date_____

Today's thoughts . . . _____

_____

_____

_____

_____

I was reminded of the Scripture that says . . . _____

_____

_____

_____

_____

How can I begin or continue to apply this verse to my life? . . .

_____

_____

_____

_____

Prayer requests . . . _____

_____

_____

_____

Answers to prayers . . . _____

_____

_____

_____

JOURNAL NOTES

*Date*_____

Today's thoughts . . . _____

_____

_____

_____

_____

I was reminded of the Scripture that says . . . _____

_____

_____

_____

_____

How can I begin or continue to apply this verse to my life? . . .

_____

_____

_____

_____

Prayer requests . . . _____

_____

_____

_____

Answers to prayers . . . _____

_____

_____

_____

JOURNAL NOTES

*Date*_____

Today's thoughts . . . _____

_____

_____

_____

_____

I was reminded of the Scripture that says . . . _____

_____

_____

_____

How can I begin or continue to apply this verse to my life? . . .

_____

_____

_____

_____

Prayer requests . . . _____

_____

_____

_____

Answers to prayers . . . _____

_____

_____

_____

JOURNAL NOTES

*Date*_____

Today's thoughts . . . _____

_____

_____

_____

_____

I was reminded of the Scripture that says . . . _____

_____

_____

_____

How can I begin or continue to apply this verse to my life? . . .

_____

_____

_____

_____

Prayer requests . . . _____

_____

_____

_____

Answers to prayers . . . _____

_____

_____

_____

JOURNAL NOTES

Date _____

Today's thoughts . . . _____

_____

_____

_____

_____

I was reminded of the Scripture that says . . . _____

_____

_____

_____

_____

How can I begin or continue to apply this verse to my life? . . .

_____

_____

_____

_____

Prayer requests . . . _____

_____

_____

_____

Answers to prayers . . . _____

_____

_____

_____

JOURNAL NOTES

*Date*_____

Today's thoughts . . . _____

_____

_____

_____

_____

I was reminded of the Scripture that says . . . _____

_____

_____

_____

_____

How can I begin or continue to apply this verse to my life? . . .

_____

_____

_____

_____

_____

Prayer requests . . . _____

_____

_____

_____

_____

Answers to prayers . . . _____

_____

_____

_____

JOURNAL NOTES

*Date*_____

Today's thoughts . . . _____

_____

_____

_____

_____

I was reminded of the Scripture that says . . . _____

_____

_____

_____

_____

How can I begin or continue to apply this verse to my life? . . .

_____

_____

_____

_____

Prayer requests . . . _____

_____

_____

_____

Answers to prayers . . . _____

_____

_____

_____

JOURNAL NOTES

*Date*_____

Today's thoughts . . . _____

_____

_____

_____

_____

I was reminded of the Scripture that says . . . _____

_____

_____

_____

_____

How can I begin or continue to apply this verse to my life? . . .

_____

_____

_____

_____

Prayer requests . . . _____

_____

_____

_____

Answers to prayers . . . _____

_____

_____

_____

JOURNAL NOTES

*Date*_____

Today's thoughts . . . _____

_____

_____

_____

_____

I was reminded of the Scripture that says . . . _____

_____

_____

_____

How can I begin or continue to apply this verse to my life? . . .

_____

_____

_____

_____

Prayer requests . . . _____

_____

_____

_____

Answers to prayers . . . _____

_____

_____

_____

NOTES

Chapter One:

1. Turning Point Ministries, *Insight Group—group member guide*, 1989, 1992, 1995.

2. William Martin, *A PROPHET WITH HONOR*: *The Billy Graham Story,* published by Quill, 1991.

3. David Barton, *America—to pray or not to pray*, 1995—published by Wallbuilder Press.

4. Shane Idleman, *What Works When "Diets" Don't,* 2002, and *What Works for Singles,* 2003—published by El Paseo Publications.

Chapter Two:

1. FOCUS ON THE FAMILY, September 2002 newsletter. Data from the National Survey of Family and Households.

2. Tommy Nelson, *The Book of Romance*, 1998—published by Thomas Nelson.

3. Shane Idleman, *What Works When "Diets" Don't,* 2002, and *What Works for Singles,* 2003—published by El Paseo Publications.

Chapter Three:

1. March/April 2003 edition of *New Man* magazine, published by Strang Communications Co., Lake Mary, Florida.

2. The Three-in-one Concise—Bible reference companion, published by Nelson, 1982

3. Charles Stanley, *Charles Stanley's handbook for Christian Living,* published by Thomas Nelson, 1996.

4. Shane Idleman, *What Works When "Diets" Don't,* 2002, and *What Works for Singles,* 2003—published by El Paseo Publications.

Chapter Four:

1. Tommy Nelson, *The Book of Romance*, 1998—published by Thomas Nelson.

2. Shane Idleman, *What Works When "Diets" Don't,* 2002, and *What Works for Singles,* 2003—published by El Paseo Publications.

Chapter Five:

1. Zig Ziglar, *Zig—the autobiography of Zig Ziglar,* published by Doubleday, New York, New York, 2002.

2. *FOCUS on the Family* magazine, 2002.

3. The Three-in-one Concise—Bible reference companion, published by Nelson, 1982.

4. Bishop T.D. Jakes at San Quinton Prison *(Tape Series: Prison Breaking Truths).*

5. Bishop T.D. Jakes, *I'll Never Do That Again-The Temptation Series, 2002.*

6. David Barton, *America—to pray or not to pray,* 1995—published by Wallbuilder Press.

7. Shane Idleman, *What Works When "Diets" Don't,* 2002, and *What Works for Singles,* 2003—published by El Paseo Publications.

Chapter Six:

1. Bob Demoss, *TV The Great Escape;* interview on Family Life Today.

2. Ted Broer, *Maximum Energy,* 1999—published by Siloam Press.

3. Shane Idleman, *What Works When "Diets" Don't,* 2002, and *What Works for Singles,* 2003—published by El Paseo Publications.

Chapter Seven:

1. Shane Idleman, *What Works When "Diets" Don't,* 2002, and *What Works for Singles,* 2003—published by El Paseo Publications.

Chapter Eight:

1. The Three-in-one Concise—Bible reference companion, published by Nelson, 1982

2. Jack Hayford, Scott Bauer and John Tolle. *Tape series entitled: The DEVASTATING Dimensions of Divorce* (SC 408).

3. Weldon Phillip Keller, *A Shepherd Looks at Psalm 23,* published by Zondervan 1970.

4. James C. Dobson, *Love Must Be Tough,* published by Word publishing, 1996.

5. Shane Idleman, *What Works When "Diets" Don't,* 2002, and *What Works for Singles,* 2003—published by El Paseo Publications.